WICCAN
WARRIOR

What is a Warrior?

A Warrior is a person who, through objective and thorough self-examination, develops an understanding of personal talents and limitations. As a Warrior, you then achieve your goals using a combination of this self-awareness and willpower to overcome weaknesses, fears, and limitations. The Wiccan Warrior's path is the Wiccan Rede in action: "An' it harm none, do what thou wilt." It is taking responsibility for your actions. It has nothing to do with being a police officer or serving in the military. It has nothing to do with being male or female. You may be a cook, a teacher, a painter, or whatever other occupation you care to name. Every Warrior is different.

Being a Warrior is daring to be more than you thought you could be. Dare to excel. Take charge of the process of change in your life—don't let the process of change take control of you. Learn to raise energy and use it effectively to bring your dreams to fruition. Be responsible and honorable. Don't settle for the status quo. Be glorious!

About the Author

A former Air Force officer, Kerr Cuhulain (Vancouver) has been a police officer for the past twenty years, and a Wiccan for thirty. He is one of the few publicly Wiccan police officers in the world. He's served on a SWAT team, Gang Crime Unit, and hostage negotiation team. He travels throughout North America as a popular speaker at writers' conferences and Pagan festivals, and he has been the subject of many books, articles, and media interviews. He is author of *The Law Enforcement Guide to Wicca*.

To Write to the Author

If you wish to contact the author or would like more information about this book, please write to the author in care of Llewellyn Worldwide and we will forward your request. Both the author and publisher appreciate hearing from you and learning of your enjoyment of this book and how it has helped you. Llewellyn Worldwide cannot guarantee that every letter written to the author can be answered, but all will be forwarded. Please write to:

Kerr Cuhulain
℅ Llewellyn Worldwide
P.O. Box 64383, Dept. K252-6
St. Paul, MN 55164-0383, U.S.A.

Please enclose a self-addressed stamped envelope for reply,
or $1.00 to cover costs. If outside U.S.A., enclose
international postal reply coupon.

WICCAN WARRIOR

WALKING A SPIRITUAL PATH IN A SOMETIMES HOSTILE WORLD

KERR CUHULAIN

Author of *The Law Enforcement Guide to Wicca*

2001
Llewellyn Publications
St. Paul, Minnesota 55164-0383 U.S.A.

FIRST EDITION
Third Printing, 2001

Book design and editing by Michael Maupin
Cover design by Anne-Marie Garrison

Library of Congress Cataloging-in-Publication Data
Cuhulain, Kerr, 1954 –
    Wiccan warrior : walking a spiritual path in a sometimes hostile world /
      Kerr Cuhulain.
        p.   cm.
    Includes bibliographical references and index.
    ISBN 1-56718-252-6
    1. Witchcraft. 2. Self-realization—Miscellanea. I. Title.
    BF1566.C83 2000
    133.4'3—dc21   99-089966

Llewellyn Publications
A Division of Llewellyn Worldwide, Ltd.
P. O. Box 64383, Dept. K252-6
St. Paul, MN 55164-0383, U.S.A.
www.llewellyn.com

Printed in the United States of America

Also by Kerr Cuhulain

The Law Enforcement Guide to Wicca
(Horned Owl Publications, Third edition, 1997)

To Phoenix:
A warrior who is my inspiration and my life.

To my friend Gil Puder:
A true warrior who did not play at life, but took Thoreau's advice and earnestly lived it from end to end. His path was truth, which, as Bruce Lee told us, is outside of all patterns.

If one man conquers in battle a thousand men, and if another conquers himself, he is the greatest of conquerors.

—The Dhammapada

CONTENTS

Introduction / xiii

INTRODUCTION

I HAVE BEEN A Witch for thirty years. Wicca is my way of life. I have been a Witch for longer than I have been a police officer, and I have been a cop for two decades. I am public about my beliefs. This makes me a bit of a curiosity, because not many police officers these days would admit to practicing Wicca. Centuries of religious persecution and intolerance by the Church have made it difficult for many Wiccans to find acceptance within Western society. Especially Wiccan cops.

This is not merely paranoia. In the years that I have been involved in antidefamation work, I have investigated reports of people losing jobs, homes, children, and even their lives as the result of modern "witch hunts." We aren't the only people affected by such discrimination, plenty of other minority groups have similar tales to tell. The spirit of the Inquisition lives on, though not as openly as it once was.

Being a cop who is public about his Wiccan beliefs has not been easy for me. I quickly found out exactly how conservative most of the police community is. That was not entirely unexpected. But I also had to overcome a lot of suspicion in the Pagan community. Initially, a lot of Wiccans thought that I was really a cop who was infiltrating the Pagan community as a sort of agent provocateur. I had to overcome a lot of resistance in both areas of my life.

About a decade ago I became heavily involved in antidefamation work. I was struggling to find a way to endure this opposition. Gradually

I learned to survive in this environment. I adopted a Wiccan path that allowed me to handle anything that my job or my life could throw at me. I came to the realization that what I had been doing before was nonproductive. I stopped writing and lecturing about antidefamation. I had found a new way to live successfully and publicly as a Wiccan in a sometimes hostile world, the way of the Wiccan Warrior.

This book is a summary of that knowledge. It won't make you just like me. We are all individuals, after all. This way is my way, and in it you may find things that may work for you, too. Hopefully you will use it to avoid the pitfalls that some of us Wiccans have encountered. Hopefully it will improve the quality of your life. I'm not looking for followers; but the world could use a few more Warriors.

Part One

THE WICCAN WARRIOR

1

What is a Warrior?

Mastering Change

Fear is the mind-killer. Fear is the little death that brings total obliteration. I will face my fear. I will permit it to pass over me and through me. And when it has gone past I will turn the inner eye to see its path. Where the fear has gone there will be nothing. Only I will remain.[1]

—Bene Gesserit Litany in Frank Herbert's *Dune*

CONFUCIUS ONCE SAID that only the supremely wise and the ignorant do not alter. Everything must change. When I decided to become a Wiccan, I accepted the idea that I had the power to cause change in conformity with my will. I embraced the belief that I was connected to the divine in the world which surrounded me, rather than being separate from it. At first, I wasn't thinking about changing myself, but change I did. My decision to become Wiccan was the first step on the path to self-transformation.

Many people just let this process of metamorphosis take them where it will. They don't notice most of the transformations in their life that come about over the years. Suddenly one day they find themselves staring at someone they don't recognize in the mirror. Often they don't like what they see. The American Indian shaman Sun Bear once said, "A lot of people are waiting for others in this world to be brave enough to do the things that they think they should be doing."[2] When most people want change, they pray for some miracle to come their way. They dream of winning the lottery, or getting the big break.

This is not the Wiccan Warrior's way. A true Warrior, as the brujo don Juan Matus often pointed out to his pupil Carlos Castaneda, has a purpose and a will. To become a Wiccan Warrior is to take charge of the process of change, to begin a journey of self-discovery and transformation. "The point of warriorship is to work personally with your situation now, as it is."[3] Never mind what you might have been (or not been) in the past. It is what you want to be that counts. Don Juan called this "throwing away your personal history."[4] A Wiccan Warrior dares to be whatever she wills.

"Change is a law, and no amount of pretending will alter that reality."[5] You will change, so why not take charge of this event? Make it a change that you want, rather than one you don't. What are your dreams? What do you want to be? Do you want to lose weight? Do you wish to quit an addiction? Do you want to get rid of old habits? Warriors use their intent and will to shape their lives. All of their actions are conscious, intentional, and complete. They strive to eliminate habitual behavior. Dan Millman's teacher Socrates gave him this advice: "Urges do not matter; actions do. Persist as a Warrior."[6]

What is a Warrior? Here's my definition: A Warrior is a person who, through objective and thorough self-examination, develops an understanding of his talents and limitations. A Warrior then achieves his goals using a combination of this self-awareness and his will to overcome weaknesses, fears, and limitations. The Wiccan Warrior's path is the Wiccan Rede in action: "An' it harm none, do what thou wilt." It is taking responsibility for your actions. It has nothing to do with being a police officer or serving in the military. It has nothing to do with being male or female. It is the process of taking charge of your life.

In the early sixteenth century, a master swordsman named Miyamoto Musashi named this path of the Warrior "Heiho" ("Path to Enlightenment"). Musashi said that "the Essence of Heiho is to build an indomitable spirit and an iron will; to believe that you cannot fail in doing anything."[7] This is the path I took on the way to my becoming a Wiccan Warrior.

I recently saw an article in a New Age magazine describing how one can become a "crystal warrior." The authors said that this was to be achieved by shooting healing power with an "autoelectromag," a sort of homemade handgun of copper and wood with a quartz crystal attached to it, or so said the article. In the article the following statements were made:

> In secret societies across the earth, the warrior became the healer, magician, and medicine man. . . . The use of swords and daggers throughout the ages has brought an understanding of the spiritual forces of creation and the individual knowledge of oneness that cannot be taught in words, but can be experienced directly by the individual. . . . What began, over and over again, as weapons of war and strife, have progressed on the path of the warrior to spiritual tools for growth, understanding—and peace.[8]

Tell that to any street gang member and take notice of the vacant stares that you'll get. I've spent twenty-one years as a police officer, in contact on a day-to-day basis with gangsters armed with, not just knives, but frequently semi- and fully automatic firearms. Their use of knives has not developed their understanding of "spiritual forces of creation." Their use of edged weapons hasn't caused them to progress. Criminals use such weapons to commit violent crimes. As a police officer, I don't carry a handgun, an Asp baton, and a canister of OC spray to become a healer and a medicine man. I carry them to protect others and simply to stay alive.

I'm quite sure that my Celtic Warrior ancestors, Vercingetorix and Boudicea, would have been surprised to hear such statements. They would not have understood the concept of "crystal warriors." They'd likely have been mystified by the idea of "weapons of war and strife" evolving into "spiritual tools for growth, understanding—and peace." Some of our modern weapons of war would have seemed as magical as an "autoelectromag" to these ancient Celts. But they wouldn't have considered such weapons tools of healing. They remain "weapons of war and strife," albeit more sophisticated ones. Having been on the receiving end of hostile gunfire several times, I can tell you that wars and weapons generally seem a lot less spiritual to those who are in the midst of battle. One's mind is on more important things at times like that, like survival.

In modern Western culture, we are surrounded by what we are told are warrior images. GI Joe stuff. Heroic Hollywood figures played by actors like Eastwood, Stallone, Willis, and Schwartzenegger. Gladiators solving all of the world's problems with fists and firearms. I'm not such an idealist that I believe that I could do my job as a police officer without occasionally using force to manage the violence of criminals. But there is a big difference between using only as much force as is necessary and the excessive force and destruction that are characteristic of these Hollywood crime dramas. If I let myself behave in this violent manner, I would be no better than the criminals that I deal with. Force isn't the answer. Too often it simply breeds more bloodshed in the form of vendetta and revenge. This Hollywood "warrior" stereotype is incomplete and unbalanced. Meditation master Chogyam Trungpa put it this way:

> Warriorship . . . does not refer to making war on others. Aggression is the source of our problems, not the solution. Here the word "warrior" is taken from the Tibetan Pawo, which literally means "one who is brave." Warriorship . . . is the tradition of human bravery, or the tradition of fearlessness.[9]

A true Warrior wins most of his battles with his head, not his hands. Two thousand years ago the Warrior-philosopher Sun Tzu gave this sound advice: "Those who win every battle are not really skillful—those who render others' armies helpless without fighting are the best of all."[10] The Samurai Warrior Musashi put it this way: The "trained martial artist . . . truly acts only in response to aggression. He does not seek it out. When made, his responses are nonresistant and nonviolent. He is a man of peace."[11]

Yet, the crystal warrior concept is just as unbalanced as this Hollywood concept of a warrior. It denies reality. Running about shooting random energy out of homemade crystal guns isn't responsible or sensible. It won't heal the destructive effects of war and ignorance. It creates a false perception of reality for the person carrying it, just like solving all of your problems with your fists. What is needed is a more balanced approach than either of these two alternatives.

"The Law of Balance states quite simply that if you wish to survive, let alone become powerful, you must keep all aspects of your universe balanced."[12] The Wiccan Warrior needs a balanced way of considered and appropriate action. We aren't going to save the world by randomly sending out energy with only a vague aim of healing. We're going to save it by changing people's perceptions of the world. We'll save it by winning hearts and minds to the idea that we can all be unique and that this is all right. We need to bring people to the realization that real power is power *with,* not power *over.* We need to make mankind realize that the earth is not ours, we are *of* the earth. We start this process by changing ourselves. We set the example.

I'm not about to give up my Berreta semi-auto handgun and Asp baton for an "autoelectromag" quartz crystal gun. But I'm also justifiably proud of the fact that I've never had to shoot anyone in twenty-one years of police work. I've used my skills to contain other people's violence, even though I spent five and a half of these years in an ERT (SWAT) Team and four of them in a Gang Crime Unit. I've used only as much force as is necessary to accomplish this end. I am a Wiccan, after all, and governed by the Wiccan Rede. I hope that someday we can change people's beliefs to the point that we don't need police and armies anymore. But the reality is that right now my job is still essential. We still need some people to manage other people's violence.

I think that what the authors of the crystal warrior article were hinting at was that over the years a few people have used their martial arts and disciplines to learn about themselves. They expanded their capabilities. They found self-respect. They discovered all of the parts that are the sum of what they were. Then they put this knowledge to good use. They learned that what should be measured is the effort that you make to improve yourself, rather than the improvements themselves. As a result, they developed a spirit of self-reliance. This is the voyage of self-discovery that you will experience in some reputable martial arts schools. This is also the way of the Wiccan Warrior. As don Juan Matus once said: "What matters to a warrior is arriving at the totality of oneself."[13]

The everyday Wiccan can experience the Warrior's path without becoming a combatant. Being a Warrior is not about fighting. It's about freeing yourself of limitations so that you can be truly creative and effective in life. "The good news is that the Warrior, properly accessed, can do a great deal to empower us to live our lives, make our worlds, and protect, provide, and create a just order on a perilous planet."[14] Following the Warrior's path won't make you the same as me. Every Warrior is unique. But every true Warrior is on the same path. Let's look more closely at that path.

Endnotes

1. Herbert, Frank. (1965) *Dune.* Berkley Publishing, New York, NY, p. 8.
2. From a presentation given by Sun Bear in California in 1985.
3. Trungpa, Chogyam. (1995) *Shambhala: The Sacred Path of the Warrior.* Shambhala, Boston, MA, p. 42.
4. Castaneda, Carlos. (1972) *Journey to Ixtlan: The Lessons of Don Juan.* Simon and Schuster, Markham, Ontario, p. 11.
5. Millman, Dan. (1984) *The Way of the Peaceful Warrior: A Book That Changes Lives.*, H. J. Kramer, Inc., Tiburton, CA, p. 61.
6. Ibid., p. 136.
7. Musashi, Miyamoto. (1988) *The Book of Five Rings.* Bantam Books, New York, NY, p. 12.
8. Smith, Michael G. and Lin Westhorp. (January/February 1993) "The Crystal Warrior." *New Worlds* magazine, Llewellyn Publications, St. Paul, MN.
9. Trungpa, p. 10.
10. Sun Tzu, trans., Thomas Cleary. (1991) *The Art of War.* Shambhala, Boston, MA, p. 18.

11. Musashi, Introduction, p. xxvii.

12. Bonewits, P. E. I. (1970) *Real Magic.* Creative Arts Book Company, Berkeley, CA, p. 10.

13. Castaneda, Carlos. (1974) *Tales of Power.* Simon & Schuster, Markham, Ontario, p. 4.

14. Moore, Robert and Douglas Gillette. (1992) *The Warrior Within: Accessing the Knight in the Male Psyche.*, HarperCollins, San Francisco, CA, p. 61.

THE WICCAN WARRIOR

"Right Action"

So it is said that if you know others and know yourself, you will not be imperiled in a hundred battles; if you do not know others but know yourself, you win one and lose one; If you do not know others and do not know yourself, you will be imperiled in every single battle.[1]

—Sun Tzu

THERE ARE MANY different archetypes within today's Pagan community: Healer, Crone, Earth Mother, and Magician, to name a few. But you don't see many examples of the Warrior. And yet I've met many Pagans who have told me that they've always wondered what it would be like to be a Warrior. Why would the average Wiccan want to connect their spirituality with Warrior principles?

I suspect that the reason that many Pagans do not access the Warrior archetype is the negative connotations that modern Pagans attach to the term. Many haven't tried to access the Warrior within because they thought that this meant becoming a man-at-arms, fighting wars and causing bloodshed. Small wonder, since many of the most barbarous acts in history were committed by people who claimed to be Warriors. Many equate Warriorship with patriarchy, as if it was an exclusively male preserve. Still others equate the Warrior archetype with unbridled rage and aggression. This isn't what being a Warrior is all about.

Each person has the Warrior inside of them. It is a personal decision as to whether you use this archetype or not. Making a connection with the Warrior inside of you is a way of accessing energy and magic that can bring many positive changes into your life. Jungian psychoanalyst Robert Moore put it this way:

> A man who appropriately accesses the archetypal Warrior draws upon enormous resources that enable him to live an empowered life in the service of his fellow creatures . . . When the Warrior is on-line, we feel a rush of blood and adrenaline, a quickening heartbeat, and a sense of something momentous about to happen. We feel mobilized for action, ready to charge forward to meet life head-on. Our daily concerns fall away from us and we are swept up into a kind of ecstacy in which we see ourselves and the world with a sharpened focus and clarity. Hidden rage is transmuted into energized courage. We come into touch with the great mystery of life and death, and we feel a strange sense of pleasure in the midst of pain.[2]

The path of the Wiccan Warrior connects martial disciplines with spirituality. There are many ancient precedents for connections of this sort. One only needs to look at the Asian martial arts to see how the philosophies of Zen Buddhism and Confucianism have been incorporated into them. To incorporate Wiccan philosophies into the Warrior tradition is not difficult. One can find many similarities in comparing modern Wiccan precepts with ancient martial philosophies.

For example, the symbol of the Wiccan religion is the five-pointed star or pentagram. Each point of the pentagram represents one of the five basic elements that form the building blocks of reality: earth, air, fire, water and spirit. Musashi's famous *Book of Five Rings (Gorin No Sho)*, a book of Warrior philosophy written in the early sixteenth century, is organized according to these same five elements: Chi No Maki (The Earth Book), Mizu No Maki (The Book of Water), Hi No Maki (The Fire Book), Kaze No Maki (The Wind Book), and Ku No Maki

(The Book of Emptiness). These five elements are the "five rings" referred to in the title of Musashi's work. Centuries earlier, Sun Tzu listed five essential considerations for the Warrior: "The five things are the way, the weather, the terrain, the leadership, and discipline."[3]

What Sun Tzu refers to here is accepting reality and working with it. This has always been the true Warrior's way. The most important aspect of a Warrior's perception of reality is honest self-evaluation. "Dishonesty to oneself is bad discipline."[4] I accept my limitations, and either make them work for me or do what I can to turn them into advantages. Each person has natural qualities and abilities as well as certain faults and limitations. For every strength there is a weakness and vice versa.[5] A Wiccan Warrior recognizes the totality of these characteristics and puts them to use in the most appropriate way. You may be a cook, a teacher, a painter, or whatever other occupation you care to name. Every Warrior is different. "It is necessary to polish your own path."[6]

And this is the way it should be. True Warriors are realists. They take what they've got and they use it effectively. Those familiar with Al-Anon's Twelve-Step Program will recognize some of the steps here:

4. Make a searching and fearless moral inventory of ourselves.

10. Continue to take personal inventory and when we were wrong promptly admitted it.

As a Wiccan Warrior I've taken responsibility for my life. I strive to create my life spontaneously rather than letting it be determined by my past, using the principles and techniques of Wicca. What I am is what I've forged with the energy I've raised and the magic that I've worked. I cause change in conformity with my will.

What does taking responsibility mean for the Wiccan Warrior? In Wicca I found that there was effectively only one law, called "The Wiccan Rede." "Rede" is a Middle English term which comes from the root word "raedan," which means "to interpret." In the second edition of *Webster's New Twentieth Century Dictionary* it is defined as, "1. counsel; advice. 2. plan, scheme. 3. a story, tale. 4. an interpretation."

A modern English translation of the Wiccan Rede would be: "Do what you will, as long as it harms no one." The Wiccan Rede is a serious responsibility. It teaches us that every action has its price. It calls upon the Wiccan to examine every one of their actions to determine their implications to others. It calls for a high level of self-discipline from every Witch. The basis of law in Western society is extensive sets of rules and regulations against which most people judge their conduct, a relatively simple process by comparison. It is not an unstructured call to self-examination like the Rede.

Some Wiccan detractors have interpreted the Wiccan Rede to mean, "Do whatever feels good." Over the years I've encountered some people at Pagan festivals and public Circles who have demonstrated by their words and deeds that they seem to have arrived at a similar interpretation. Those who have the least to lose by being public are usually the first to go public. Unfortunately these sort of irresponsible public antics have sometimes made it very difficult for those of us with a lot to lose to follow suit.

The moment I became a cop I put myself under a spotlight of public scrutiny. The moment that I became public about being a Wiccan, this scrutiny was intensified. After all, people have been bombarded with propaganda about Witches being Satanists for years. So it was only natural to expect my department, and the public, to examine me closely and at length to see if I was really some dangerous Satanic cult member. In my case, I knew that the only way that these people could reassure themselves was to allow them to investigate me. The greater the responsibility attached to your profession, the greater the likelihood that scrutiny of this sort will be turned in your direction.

As a Wiccan Warrior, I accept this. A Warrior must be impeccable. To earn respect, you must make yourself respectable. This has meant a certain amount of sacrifice for me. I suppose I could easily have felt sorry for myself for being subjected to such scrutiny and attention. I could have called such treatment unfair and unjust. Others in my place might have felt themselves to be at the mercy of the fates; or would have felt this way, if they did not take responsibility for their actions as a Warrior should. "A warrior takes his lot, whatever it may be, and accepts it in ultimate humbleness. He accepts in humbleness what he is, not as grounds for regret, but as a living challenge."[7] I don't seek pain and frustration. But if they come, a Warrior puts them to use.

This brings to mind two more of Al-Anon's Twelve Steps:

> 8. Make a list of all persons we had harmed and became willing to make amends to them all.

> 9. Made direct amends to such people wherever possible except when to do so would injure them or others.

If my actions unexpectedly result in a harmful conclusion, I do my best to make it right again. I don't try to lay the blame on others. Saying I'm sorry is a start, but by itself it is not enough. Praying, making secret confessions, or paying alms to some deity or church may ease your conscience. But it doesn't make you more responsible and often it does not correct the problem that you created in the first place. It simply gives you a way out, a way to avoid responsibility. Accountability is an absolute necessity for a Warrior. It is a sacred trust that allows you to learn from your mistakes.

I am *not* saying here that Wiccan Warriors must be public about their beliefs. I am not suggesting that Wiccan Warriors should all become involved in antidefamation work or public demonstrations. What I am saying is that the Wiccan Warrior examines the circumstances of his or her life, and makes informed, realistic decisions based on the facts available. Wiccan Warriors must thoroughly evaluate the neighborhood in which they reside to determine if the risks of being public outweigh the possible gains. If you're a solitary Wiccan in a predominantly Bible-belt town, being public might not be such a wise idea. Sun Tzu once said: "Good warriors take their stand on ground where they cannot lose."[8]

This doesn't make you any less of a Warrior. Warriors don't take stupid risks. Don Juan Matus cautions us: "A warrior . . . cuts to a minimum his chances of the unforeseen . . . [he lives] strategically."[9] It is not a matter of a Warrior being fearless. Only fools do not fear. But the

Warrior faces his fears and deals with them. "True fearlessness is not the reduction of fear, but going beyond fear."[10]

A friend of mine, Paul Tuitean, once told me that the difference between a soldier and a Warrior is that "soldiers march and Warriors dance." Warriors dance along the knife edge, maintaining balance of their totality. They celebrate their strength while keeping rigidly under control, only bringing it to bear when it is appropriate and unavoidable. There is an old principle in Aikido: When pushed, you pull; when pulled, you push; you find the natural course and bend with it.

This does not mean that you simply let yourself be governed by impulses. A Warrior thinks before acting, but it's not just a matter of thinking either. Some people say that it has to do with honor. *Webster's New Twentieth Century Dictionary* defines honor as "a sense of what is right, just and true; dignified respect for character, springing from probity, principle, or moral rectitude." The Wiccan Warrior must develop a fine sense of what's called "right action." Simply stated, right action is "what is right, just and true."

What is "right action" for the Wiccan Warrior? It's a sum of all of the things discussed in this chapter. A Wiccan accesses the Warrior archetype by accepting reality and making a thorough self-examination. Right action is accepting the Wiccan rede and the self-discipline and responsibility that it evokes. It's about earning respect and facing your fears. And how does the Wiccan Warrior accomplish these things? In the next chapter we'll discuss how Warriors use the principles of monism, openness, and Karma to empower themselves.

Endnotes

1. Sun Tzu, trans., Thomas Cleary. (1991) *The Art of War.* Shambhala, Boston, MA, p. 24.

2. Moore, Robert and Douglas Gillette. (1992) *The Warrior Within: Accessing the Knight in the Male Psyche.* HarperCollins, San Francisco, CA, p. 100.

3. Sun Tzu, p. 2.

4. Musashi, Miyamoto. (1988) *The Book of Five Rings.* Bantam Books, New York, NY, p. 30.

5. Millman, Dan. (1984) *The Way of the Peaceful Warrior: A Book That Changes Lives.* H. J. Kramer, Inc., Tiburton, CA, p. 184.

6. Musashi, p. 21.

7. Castaneda, Carlos. (1974) *Tales of Power.* Simon & Schuster, Markham, Ontario, p. 19.

8. Sun Tzu, p. 29.

9. Castaneda, Carlos. (1976) *A Separate Reality: Further Conversations with Don Juan.* Simon & Schuster, Markham, Ontario, p. 182.

10. Trungpa, Chogyam. (1995) *Shambhala: The Sacred Path of the Warrior.* Shambhala, Boston, MA, p. 48.

3

THE BALANCED WARRIOR

Monism, Openness, and Karma

Our word religion comes from the Latin and means "to bind together." A successful religion is one that binds together all the fundamental rhythms that each of us experiences: the personal rhythm of the human body, the larger social rhythm of the family, tribe, or nation, and the enveloping cosmic rhythms of the planet and the universe. If the religion "works," its followers are rewarded by a new dimension of rhythm and time—the sacred.[1]

—Mickey Hart

THE WICCAN WARRIOR is inextricably linked to the earth; a monist. She sees that divinity is immanent in everything. Everything is sacred. The Wiccan Warrior knows that she can have paradise here and now. Divinity *cannot* be separated from the everyday world. It is an integral part of it. This is the meaning behind the expression "Thou art God/dess," or what Buddha meant when he said, "Look within, thou art the Buddha." When I look at you, I recognize that you are one of the many reflections of deity in the world. The Gods are everywhere, in everything. Jesus said, "The kingdom of Heaven is within you." He was right.

When a dualistic person looks at a tree, they see an object. A certain number of board feet of lumber. Something that can be used to build a church, or make a profit. When I look at a tree, I see a living organism.

Something to be respected and revered. Something that has as much right to be here as I do. Something sacred. Something connected to me. If it must be used, it must be used wisely. Only as much as is needed is taken. I see that it is eventually replaced with another tree and I give proper thanks for its use. Thus, the delicate balance is maintained. It is the difference between being a ruler and a steward. The earth is not ours; we are *of* the earth. Everything is connected.

The Wiccan Warrior holds everything in the land sacred, unified, and in harmony, and considers himself part of it. If you've ever looked at Celtic art, you'll note that a lot of it is complex interlocking knots and designs. This reflects the Celtic belief that everything in life is linked together with interwoven patterns of energy. If the pattern is maintained, all is well. If it is disturbed, the balance is upset and things go wrong.

This is an extremely important concept to the Wiccan Warrior. If you want to work magick or practice martial arts effectively, you must understand this connectedness, this balance. The martial artist and the skilled magician have this in common: balance is crucial. A real Warrior needs no strength at all to defeat an opponent who is off balance. The tiniest shove or pull in the right place is sufficient to bring the opponent down. This is what allows the skilled martial artist (or cop like me) to control violent people with a minimum of force. You learn how to put the opponent off balance while maintaining your own equilibrium.

So it is with magick. A Wiccan Warrior only needs to apply the tiniest amount of energy to the right place to affect the whole interconnected system around them. "Sorcery is to apply one's will to a key joint,"[2] don Juan Matus once told his student Carlos Castaneda. Castaneda relates an anecdote in which don Juan magickally prevents Carlos from starting the engine of his vehicle by applying his will to the sparkplugs.[3] He chose this key joint of the engine and applied his will to it.

Some Wiccans of my acquaintance put a great deal of emphasis on raising enormous amounts of energy and very little (if any) on using that energy effectively. Remember the story of David and Goliath? Bigger isn't necessarily better. Energetic rituals are fine, but they aren't truly powerful unless that energy is properly used. In Hollywood action dramas, combatants use exaggerated, leaping roundhouse kicks and conspicuous punches to defeat their opponents. The scene is more dramatic that way, but it is just acting. In real life the opposite is true: The most effective martial arts moves are the ones that are so subtle they are hard to see. Martial artist and actor Bruce Lee was very good at displaying these flashy moves for the camera. But one of his most impressive martial arts demonstrations off-screen was his "one-inch punch." He would hold his fist against his assistant's chest, withdraw it just one inch, and punch with sufficient force to drop this assistant flat. Strength was only a tiny part of the equation; energy, or Chi, supplied the rest. We'll return to the techniques of energy use later in this book. For now let's explore these concepts of balance and interconnectedness a little further.

Many religions use guilt to dominate people. Followers are made to feel unworthy and taught that failure is an inevitable human quality. The dualistic concept of "original sin" is often used for this purpose. Followers are taught that the only way to save themselves is through constant confession of their failings, which will bring about their redemption. Many fundamentalist Christians teach that no matter how good a person you are, unless you believe in Jesus, their compassionate God will send you to Hell.

The Wiccan Warrior isn't immune to failure. But a Warrior does not succumb to guilt. Critic Cyril Connolly once wrote:

> When I contemplate the accumulation of guilt and remorse which, like a garbage-can, I carry through life, and which is fed not only by the lightest action but by the most harmless pleasure, I feel Man to be of all living things the most biologically incompetent and ill-organized. Why has he acquired a seventy year's life-span only to poison it incurably by the mere being of himself? Why had he thrown Conscience, like a dead rat, to putrefy in the well?[4]

The Wiccan Warrior realizes we all have individual characteristics that, in different circumstances, may be assets or liabilities. Wiccan Warriors examine themselves and learn to use their individual characteristics to succeed. They try to learn from their mistakes and celebrate their successes and their lives. Guilt is eliminated and replaced with the Wiccan Rede. My actions are *my* responsibility. If I screw up, I fix it. To the Wiccan Warrior that counts as a victory, something she can celebrate.

Another important principle for the Wiccan Warrior is the threefold law of return. Everything being interconnected and in balance, if you do good things, even more good things will happen to you. If you upset the balance and do evil things, many unpleasant things will happen to you. You get out more than what you put in.

This is related to the Eastern concept of Karma. Karma translates as "action," and could be simply defined as "every action has its consequences." So both Karma and this threefold law are both an integral part of the Wiccan Rede. To the Wiccan Warrior this means consequences here and now, not in some future life, as it is in some Eastern systems of belief. The Warrior lives in the *now*, directly experiencing the present moment. Now is the time for action. Now is the time to experience the fruits of that action.

Recently I've noticed some unbalanced practices within the Pagan community. There are those who believe that power is a personal thing, that power is to be hoarded. Pagans who believe that you must not reveal all of your secrets to the uninitiated (or even many of the initiated) as you will somehow diminish your personal power by doing so. I've even encountered a few stodgy "old-guard" Wiccans who have assured me that certain "mysteries of the ancients" have been deliberately left out of their Book of Shadows and are known only to them. Of course, this allows them to dole this "arcane lore" out to favored students at their discretion.

Neither energy that I raise nor the power that results from it belong to me or anyone else. We're all simply tapping in to the vast universe around us. You can't hoard something that doesn't belong to you. Becoming more masterful isn't a matter of stockpiling power. For the Wiccan Warrior, mastery is a matter of learning to use the power available to everyone more effectively. Power isn't something that you own; it's something that you achieve.

Some Wiccans who hold to this "power shared is power lost" theory have criticized me for taking this position. They don't like people like me questioning what they've accepted as "gospel" up to now. It threatens their illusions of personal power. The most common explanations that I have been given by those trying to justify the withholding of information from those of lesser degrees include:

1. You must not reveal all of your secrets to the others as, if you do, you will have given all of your power away to them.

2. They aren't ready for this information yet. They won't get it until I decide that they are worthy of/ready for it.

3. It's a third-degree mystery.

4. One of the Ordains in the Book of Shadows tells us: "So let it be ordained, that none but the Wicca may see our Mysteries, for our enemies are many."[5]

Many traditions of Wicca include rules and ordains like these demanding secrecy in their Book of Shadows. Even the name of the book suggests that this should be so. More than once I have heard people using excuses like these to justify their inability to explain something to a novice. Too often people have suggested that the subject is something known only to the highest initiates, and which cannot be revealed to the vulgar. If the leader of a group that you have joined is withholding information from you and cannot give a better reason than those I've listed above, maybe you should look more closely at them. Are they doing this to create the impression that they know more than they really do? Are they doing this to create an atmosphere about themselves to which they have no legitimate claim? Are they hoping to hide from you the fact that they really don't know much more about the Craft than you do? If they are, get out. You are not in a coven. You are participating in a cult group.

When you take a course at a college or university, they give you textbooks with all of the course information in them. You start at the beginning and work through the course material, hopefully attaining a mastery of it as you progress. But, at any time, you can flip ahead through the pages to see what comes next. At any time you can go to the library to look up other aspects of the subject that you are studying. Nothing about what you are studying is secret or occult. Your professor is your teacher because they are recognized as an authority on a particular subject, not because they are hoarding secret lore.

The term priest comes from the Anglo Saxon word "preost," derived from a Latin term "presbyter" ("elder"). That is what I now am. As an elder, I pass on my knowledge to newer Wiccans so that they, in turn, can experience the same things. Hopefully they will eventually become elders themselves, ready to teach the next generation. As a Wiccan Warrior I don't interpret, I point out the possible paths. The general teaches the soldier to follow orders and let headquarters do the thinking. The Warrior teaches the novice to think for themselves. I am reminded of the scene in the movie *Braveheart* in which uncle Argyle is speaking to the young William Wallace. "First I'll teach you how to use this," he says, tapping William on the head with his finger. "Then I'll teach you how to use this," he continues, showing William his broadsword.

Most Books of Shadows include an Ordain that states that Wiccans should "combat the untruths, and to spread truth about the Craft to those outside the Craft."[6] When I went public, I found myself surrounded by people asking me questions about my beliefs. How could I tell people the truth about myself if some Ordain prohibited my freedom of speech? If I couldn't tell them what I did, wouldn't it look as if I was hiding something? How can you call yourself a teacher if you can't teach all that you know? The Wiccan Warrior practices honesty and openness.

Let's not confuse being in the closet with the secrecy traditionally associated with many esoteric lodges and a few Wiccan traditions. There was a time when many of those who were members of such groups held that their beliefs should be kept secret from the public. Some still do. That's where Ordains like these originally came from. That's how their body of knowledge became known as "the occult." The word "occult" was derived from the Latin word "occultus" ("concealed"). As the word implies, it concerns information being kept secret from the public.

Occasionally this secrecy was used to create an air of mystery. Too often it came about as an attempt by a select few to hoard knowledge. This put these few in a position to dictate what people should or should not be allowed to know. Knowledge made inaccessible in order to maintain a position of power over others. But as Dion Fortune so aptly put it forty years ago:

> As so much has already been made known concerning the esoteric teachings, and as the circle of students of the occult is becoming rapidly wider every day, it may well be that the time has come for plain speaking.[7]

This is even more true now than it was when Fortune first set it down in writing. Since 1949, when Gerald Gardner wrote his novel *High Magic's Aid,* so many books have published previously secret rituals that it is not possible to make a claim to "secret knowledge" anymore. The occult isn't really occult these days.

Again, I am not saying that every Wiccan must be public about their beliefs. Common sense and circumstances will dictate the best course of action for each Wiccan. The point is that every action that you take as a Wiccan Warrior should have a purpose. I didn't see that secrecy about my beliefs had any legitimate purpose in my circumstances. It's hard to be public without being public all the way. The more that you keep from the public's view, the greater the risk that this will be perceived as hiding something shameful or illegal. This is exactly the argument presented by many of our critics. They say we are up to something clandestine. We shouldn't be blindly observing this secrecy about our beliefs out of habit or because it is directed by an Ordain in a book.

This doesn't mean that all of the Wiccan Ordains have no meaning either. The Ordains also say that "no one shall tell anyone not of the Craft who be of the Wicca, nor give any names, where they hide, or in any way tell anything which can betray us to our foes. Nor may he tell where the covendom be, or the covenstead, or where the meetings be."[8] This is just good common sense if revealing this information to others may end up causing harm to others. A Wiccan Warrior remembers the Wiccan Rede.

A Wiccan Warrior's understanding of the interconnectedness and balance of the universe around them allows them to achieve startling results with a minimum of energy expenditure. They realize that the rewards and consequences of their actions occur in the present. They become powerful by achieving mastery, not by falling prey to the illusion that power must be hoarded. Practicing honesty and openness both with themselves and those around them, they banish guilt and live fearlessly. This openness frees the mind to explore new perspectives. In the next chapter we'll use these new perspectives to examine our mythology.

Endnotes

1. Hart, Mickey. (1991) *Planet Drum*. HarperCollins, San Francisco, p. 17.
2. Castaneda, Carlos. (1976) *A Separate Reality: Further Conversations with Don Juan*. Simon & Schuster, Markham, Ontario, p. 199.
3. Ibid.
4. Connolly, Cyril. (1944; rev. 1951) *The Unquiet Grave, Part 1*. Taken from the *Columbia Dictionary of Quotations,* ©1993, Columbia University Press.
5. Georgian Book of Shadows, 13th Ordain.
6. Manifesto of the Georgians, 5th article.
7. Fortune, Dion. (1981) *Psychic Self-Defense*. The Aquarian Press, Wellingborough, UK, p. 9.
8. Georgian Book of Shadows, 15th Ordain.

4

THE CREATIVE WARRIOR

Making Mythology Work for You

Only here, in life on earth, where opposites clash together, can the general level of consciousness be raised. That seems to be man's metaphysical task—which he cannot accomplish without "mythologizing." Myth is the natural and indisputable intermediate stage between unconscious and conscious cognition. True, the unconscious knows more than the consciousness does; but it is knowledge of a special sort, knowledge in eternity, usually without reference to the here and now, not couched in the language of the intellect.[1]

—Carl Jung

INSTITUTIONS AND TRADITIONS may give a sense of permanence to a person's life. They make people comfortable and too often they remove the necessity for people to think. You do a thing because that's the way it has always been done. At the outset this may have been the result of a well-thought-out scheme, or even the result of trial and error. At one time it may have been functional, and it still may be functional.

Life involves change. And that change may make institutions and traditions obsolete. We shouldn't be doing things because they've always been done that way; the Warrior does things a particular way because that way brings results. If the traditional way doesn't work anymore, the Warrior seeks alternatives. Musashi put it this way, "This is because in the path of Heiho one cannot be so rigid as to insist that 'this is the way it has been since ancient times,' or 'this is the modern way to do it.' The path to victory lies in manipulating the circumstances so that they are to the disadvantage of the opponent."[2] A few years ago Sun Bear advised us, "The first step, on your path to power, is to look at the system, all the glitter, glamour, and neon, and say 'I don't believe it.'"[3]

A Warrior must be innovative, objective, and creative. "Victory . . . is not repetitious, but adapts its form endlessly."[4] Throughout the history of warfare one finds examples of armies of superior size being defeated by smaller groups using innovative tactics. The battles of Agincourt, Bannockburn, Cannae, Crécy, Leuthen, Marathon, Panipat, and Poitiers are just a few examples of this. Someone tries something that has never been done before and the unexpected brings victory. Often the victor had taken a fresh look at something commonplace and came up with a new perspective. Sun Tzu wrote, "Those skilled at the unorthodox are infinite as heaven and earth, inexhaustible as the great rivers. When they come to an end, they begin again, like the days and months; they die and are reborn, like the four seasons."[5]

The Wiccan Warrior is an inquisitive realist. She must be honest with herself and others. She must ask questions. The only way for our belief system to be functional is for us to be honest about our origins and to be diligent in our study. If we are not honest about our origins, then what else will we be willing to compromise? If we can be honest, we can be effective, because this will make us objective. This allows us to seek out those things that work for us and discard those that do not. This is the Warrior's way. The things that work for you may be different from those that work for me, but this is as it should be. We are individuals, not clones.

History is often written to suit those writing it, constructing selected facts to fit a preconceived idea. Most Wiccans won't argue with this statement. They have seen how the Christian religion of the majority has often influenced how Western history was recorded. They will agree that it is possible to do your homework and write an objective historical account based on the evidence available, and a growing number of historians are attempting to do just this. But, as Stuart Piggot observes, "What, however, can also be constructed is that very dangerous thing, a past-as-wished-for, in which a convenient selection of the evidence is fitted into a predetermined intellectual or emotional pattern."[6] Wiccans are as susceptible to this as anyone, and one does not have to look very far to find examples of this.

All religions were started by people, for it is people that they serve. The Wiccan religion is no exception. The early Wiccan authors, beginning with Gerald Gardner, presented a picture of a rediscovered ancient religion, which had been preserved by isolated underground groups for years and had now surfaced more or less intact. As Aidan Kelly has observed, this is a pretty typical characteristic of religions, including Judaism and Christianity.

Before going any further, I must emphasize that a historical basis is not the important issue for me. Whether or not the historical records presented by a religious group are accurate has little to do with how the religion functions or how the religion meets people's needs. Wicca, like every other religion on this earth, is based on mythology. Mythology isn't meant to be taken as literally true, though much of it has some kernel of historical truth that may serve as its basis. Mythology is metaphor and allegory, a powerful set of archetypes and symbols. Religion is mythology in action. As my wife Phoenix McFarland so aptly describes it, "Myth is the address of magick."

The Wiccan Warrior recognizes the power of their mythology, making its full power available to them. Those who fall into the trap of shifting their emphasis from the substance to the form of the religion interpret myths as historical accounts that are literally true. When this happens, the mythology will cease to function for them. Wiccan Priestess Kate Slater once wrote:

> There are three useful patterns of developing our Craft. The first and most free is to create—to extemporize or write wholly new customs and rituals as our gift to the Deities. The other patterns place emphasis on the old: They look to what little we can know of the past but differ in the amount of interpretation they allow. The

second path takes the most optimistic interpretations of the fragments we have, and builds new structures— whether on Leland's *Aradia* or on thousands of clay figures from lost civilizations. The third path is more cautious, also building on fragments, folklore and anthropology, but allowing us much less leeway to channel understanding about the distant past.[7]

The Wiccan religion binds together mythology, the cycles of nature and the seasons, and community to create a specific sacred experience. That experience will differ from one individual to the next, from one coven to another. This is how it should be. Yet too often these days I see Wiccans treating their coven's Book of Shadows like "scripture." As if it was the word of the Gods as passed down by some prophet. Too often these days I see individuals hung up on establishing their credentials, taking great pains to trace the initiations of their initiators and their initiator's initiators back in an apostolic succession to some individual like Gerald Gardner. Too often I see established groups turning up their noses at solitary Wiccans, simply because they haven't had an "approved" initiation. Too often I see groups condemning other Wiccan groups because they are doing something different from their interpretation of Wicca as presented in Gardner's Book of Shadows. This is the beginning of that institutionalization that I alluded to at the beginning of this chapter. We are beginning to see Wiccan "fundamentalists." Have you ever seen the bumper sticker that says "Born Again Pagan"? It's amusing at first glance, but in light of some people's behavior recently, it gives me the chills.

Some elements that have been assembled to form the basis of the modern Wiccan beliefs are quite old. Some go back thousands of years. But while individual practices are indeed ancient, modern Wicca is a new combination of these practices and is quite different from ancient Pagan religion in some ways.

This is as it should be. I believe that one of the greatest gifts that Wicca offers me is the gift of creativity. This is a true Warrior's gift. It is this creativity that attracts many people to Wicca, it meets the needs of many people. This imaginative element gives it the ability to grow and adapt to meet these needs. One of the problems faced by mainstream, orthodox religions these days is that their congregations are *not* growing, and cling to value systems created thousands of years ago. They haven't entertained the idea that many of these values, considered appropriate by them centuries ago, may no longer be appropriate in today's world. Rather than change to meet the necessities and needs of modern people, they choose to cling to their dogma. Remember that change is a law of nature. Change is the Warrior's way.

I've noticed that some Wiccans get very uncomfortable with this argument because they really would like to believe that Wicca can be traced back to some "Golden Age." They get very upset when certain people argue that Gerald Gardner, considered by many to be the father of modern Wicca, "invented" a religion. The problem with this argument is that every religion in history had a starting point. It was "invented" by someone, somewhere. Phoenix McFarland views it this way: "Religions are invented from shards of older practices. In an archeology dig, we find that one building is built upon the ruins of an older one. Our mythologies, like the phoenix, rise from the ashes of dying faiths. It is part of the circle of life." You don't need to go very far to find an example. It is a well-known and provable fact that the Christian church incorporated many old Pagan customs into their worship in its earlier years. Isn't this "inventing" religion?

Theologians who resort to this "older is better" argument are presenting the age-old and fallacious argument that their religion is better, because if Gardner "invented" Wicca in the 1930s, then religions like Christianity, Islam, or Judaism are older, that their religion is better because it can be traced back to some mythical "Golden Age." They are suggesting that a given religion is more valid simply because it may be older. Obviously the reason that this argument is invalid is because truth is truth, whether it was discovered five minutes ago or a thousand years ago. Truth is timeless. Age has nothing to do with it!

Not only is this "older is better" argument untrue, it is an example of power over thinking. My religion isn't "better" than any other religion. It works for me, therefore it is better for me. Each person should find the belief that works best for them. The Wiccan Warrior who practices power with would say that there is something of value to be learned along all paths. If you deny the fact that your religion was "invented," you are denying yourself a very powerful tool. You can invent your own religion. You can fine-tune it to make it work better for you. This is the way of the Wiccan Warrior.

This is exactly what the founder of modern Wicca, Gerald Gardner, did when he first started writing and publishing his now famous books on the Wiccan religion. He created a religion that contained the elements that worked for him. A new tradition of Witchcraft sprang into being, taking its name from its founder: Gardnerian Wicca. Presently others took up their pens: Raymond Buckland, Doreen Valiente, Sybil Leek, Alex Sanders, and Patricia Crowther, to name just a few. They wrote variations on the Gardnerian pattern, but they all added their own elements to make it better fit their circumstances. I won't go into this in any greater detail here. I would refer the reader to books such as Jeffrey B. Russell's *A History of Witchcraft*, Aidan Kelly's *Crafting the Art of Magic* and Ronald Hutton's *The Pagan Religions of the Ancient British Isles*. These authors have covered this in much greater detail than I am prepared to here.

Examination of Gardner's early Books of Shadows (he went through at least four revisions) shows that he pieced together his modern form of Witchcraft from various fragments. He borrowed elements from the works of Margaret Murray:

1. The terms "Old Religion," "Sabbat," and "Esbat."

2. The organization of covens into groups of thirteen.

3. The concept that Witchcraft was a religion primarily concerned with fertility.

Still others were borrowed from Charles Geoffrey Leland's book *Aradia: Gospel of the Witches*. This book was written in 1899 by Charles Leland, a lawyer and soldier of fortune. This was allegedly a description of traditional Tuscan witchcraft as described to Leland by a witch named Maddelena and a translation of their "gospel," which he named "Vangelo." It bears a striking resemblance to Michelet's earlier book *La Sorciere* (whose English translation is *Satanism and Witchcraft*).

Originally Herodias was the name of the goddess in both Leland's and Michelet's books. Michelet had accepted a theory advanced by Jarcke, Mone, Murray, and others that there had been a large, organized "Witch cult" or Pagan religion that was spread across Western Europe, under a Christian ruling class. Michelet believed that the name of the Goddess of this ancient religion was "Herodias." This happens to be the name of a very wicked woman who appears in Matthew 14:3, 14:6; Mark 6:17, 6:19, 6:22; and Luke 3:19 in the New Testament of the Bible.

In the tenth century, the Church issued the *Canon Episcopi*, which claimed that literal belief in witchcraft was folly because it was an illusion inspired by Satan. The Canon, re-enacted several times until the Council of Treves in 1310, gave the name Herodias as the name of the leader of the "Wild Hunt," the nocturnal procession of the Goddess of the Hunt and her retinue. Michelet probably thought that this was based on factual accounts, rather than the speculation of Church theologians. Leland borrowed the name Herodias from Michelet. Once rendered into Italian "Herodias" became "Aradia." The problems with Leland's allegations are that: 1. No historian or folklorist has found any evidence of the Tuscan Witch cult described by Leland, nor any evidence of a goddess named "Aradia." Leland's original use of the name "Herodias" clearly shows that he was borrowing from Michelet, or the *Canon Episcopi*, or the Bible; and, 2. The language of "Vangelo," the Witch "gospel" allegedly recovered by Leland, is unmistakably nineteenth century, and not fourteenth century as Leland suggests.

Nevertheless, Gardner borrowed Leland's idea that Aradia was a traditional Tuscan goddess. Other elements that Gardner borrowed from Leland include:

1. Probably the idea that Witchcraft, as he reported it, had survived in secret.

2. The original "Charge of the Goddess" used by Gardner. Gardner's original version was a pastiche combining excerpts from Leland's *Aradia* and Crowley's *Liber Legis*. This was later rewritten by Doreen Valiente to become the more familiar (and beautiful) modern version.

3. The concept of ritual nudity (skyclad worship). Gardner, a practicing nudist, may have gotten this idea from Leland's *Aradia*. But if you look at the European woodcuts, drawings, and prints of "Witches" from the period of the Inquisition, you'll note that Witches were normally depicted as naked in their rites, so this could as easily have given Gardner the idea.

Many elements of magick that Gardner incorporated into his tradition of Witchcraft he derived from Occidental Ceremonial Magick. Gardner, like many others at the time, probably believed that these elements were fragments of older Pagan magick. While many hundreds of years old, these originated primarily in Christian rather than Celtic culture. Sources used by Gardner included the grimoire called *The Greater Key of Solomon*. Examples of elements that Gardner borrowed from this text include:

1. The symbolic scourging.

2. The use of pentagrams and triangles as symbols.

3. The appeals to the guardians of the four cardinal directions of the Circle in Circle casting.

4. The methods for making and consecrating ritual tools.

5. Details concerning the preparation for ritual.

6. Details concerning the drawing of a magickal Circle.

7. The use of a sword and two knives, one with a black handle and one with a white handle, as well as the name of these ritual knives: the athame and the bolline.

Gardner borrowed a great many ideas from the Freemasons, such as the initiation in which the initiate is bound and blindfolded and challenged with a knife.

Gardner borrowed one well-known Wiccan chant straight out of a thirteenth-century story. Most Wiccans will recognize the chant:

Eko Eko Azarak,
Eko Eko Zomelek,
Eko Eko Arida,
Eko Eko Kernunnos,
Bezabi, Lacha, Bachababa,
Lamach, Cahi, Achababa,
Karrelos, Cahi, Achababa,
Lamach Lamach Bacharous,
Carbahaji, Sabalyos,
Barylos.
Lazos, Athame, Calyolas,
Samahac et Famyolas,
Harrahya![8]

In the fourth line, students of Celtic religion will recognize the name Kernunnos as a Gaulish god of nature. The name Arida in the third line is a variation on the name of the Goddess Aradia from Leland's book. However, most Pagans don't realize that all but the first four lines of this chant come from the book *Le Miracle de Theophile,* by the thirteenth-century trouvère Ruteboeuf. It was an incantation chanted by a sorcerer named Salatinin in this book, who was trying to conjure the Devil![9]

The Gardnerian third-degree Great Rite Ritual is obviously derived from The Gnostic Mass published by Aleister Crowley's Argentium Astrum in *Liber XV: Ecclesiae Gnosticae Catholicae Canon Missae.* This was published as part of Aleister Crowley's book *The Blue Equinox.* James Branch Cabell used this Gnostic mass in his 1919 novel *Jurgen* as the basis of a wedding ceremony involving a Goddess. Other elements that Gardner incorporated into his original Book of Shadows from the works of Crowley include:

1. The ritual of the pentagram.

2. Particulars on the use of the scourge, athame, and chain.

3. A passage on "The Bloody Sacrifice."

The spirits and deities named in Gardner's "Book of Shadows" are a mixture including:

1. Names of Hebrew demons from medieval grimoires translated by Liddell MacGregor Mathers.

2. Egyptian deities, possibly the influence of groups such as the Fellowship of Isis or the Hermetic Order of the Golden Dawn.

3. Aradia, a fictitious goddess from Leland's book.

4. Roman goddesses and gods, such as Diana.

5. Figures from Celtic mythology and literature, such as Cernunnos and Herne.

There is even a poem by Rudyard Kipling included in Gardner's Beltaine ritual:

> O do not tell the priests of our arts.
> For they would call it sin,
> For we will be in the woods all night
> A conjuring summer in.
> And we bring you good news by word of mouth
> For women, cattle, and corn:
> The sun is coming up from the south,
> With oak and ash and thorn.[10]

Gerald Gardner even added some original elements of his own; for example, the "five-fold kiss" in the Gardnerian initiation ceremony. Indeed, his unique combination of elements from diverse sources could be considered an original concept itself.

There were some aspects of ancient Pagan religion that we can be very glad Gardner did *not* include in his new religion:

1. Modern Wicca totally lacks any form of animal or human sacrifice in its practices. Such sacrifice was an aspect of many ancient religions: they believed that they obtained favors or rewards from the gods by making pleasing offerings to them. Wiccans recognize today that this

is inappropriate and unnecessary, since divinity is a part of us. This is one custom that we can be glad was *not* inherited from our ancestors.

2. Modern Wicca is essentially ditheistic: it sees the many different gods and goddesses as aspects of one goddess and one god. This is quite different from the polytheism of some ancient cultures, who usually considered these deities to be quite separate, and their own to be the mightiest.

So you can see that Gardner was clearly using that creativity I prize so highly when he wrote (and rewrote) his first Book of Shadows decades ago. He did the best he could, given the facts available to him at the time. Gardner was a revisionist or revivalist who created a Pagan religion that has since proved to be a vital and growing one. If such creativity worked for him, it can work for you, too.

Like Gardner, I was motivated to seek out the roots of modern Witchcraft. This was for me, after all, a Warrior's voyage of discovery. I thoroughly examined the elements Gardner had incorporated into his original Book of Shadows. I examined all of the Wiccan books that I could lay my hands on. I learned that the many older Wiccan how-to books based on early Gardnerian literature had Wiccans invoking obscure entities from medieval grimoires in the midst of rituals based on disproved historical assumptions or copied from traditions of Occidental (Christian) Magick. These rituals include invocations which turn out to be invocations of demons borrowed from ancient novels, interspersed with poetry borrowed from Kipling.

I felt that I could do better than this with what was now available to me. For a system of ritual and magick to be effective, it has to be well thought out and, above all, consistent. A lot of the old Wiccan stuff apparently was not. As the foundation for my beliefs was Celtic, I began looking at my practice of Wicca from a Celtic point of view. For example, I determined that the practices of the Gardnerian tradition of Wicca that *can* be traced back to ancient Pagan religion and customs include:

1. The celebration of the four Celtic cross-quarter days as festivals (Samhain, Imbolc, Beltaine, Lughnasad).

2. The celebration of the equinoxes and solstices as "lesser Sabbats," following ancient Saxon customs.

3. The name of the Wiccan wedding ceremony, "handfasting."

4. Certain rites, such as "leaping over fires."

5. The practice of dividing the Wiccan ritual circle into quarters aligned to the cardinal directions.

6. The concept of triple aspects of a deity, like that of the Gaulish Matronae, the triple aspects of the Celtic goddess Morrigan, or the three Norns (the Norse equivalent of the three Greek Moirae or "Fates").

7. The concept of calling the place to which the deceased go to rest prior to reincarnation the "Summerland." One name of the Otherworld in Celtic mythology is the "Land of Summer."

I noted that these elements were primarily drawn from Celtic and Saxon folklore. Since this Celtic heritage interested me, I used this as a basis. I went on to look at the structure of religion and Celtic religion in particular, using some more modern, proven sources. I developed my own Celtic system of Wicca that works very well for me. Since then I've tried lots of variations and found all kinds of other patterns that also work. My wife and I now invoke many different deities from many different cultures in our rituals. For example, you can see in this book how I've now incorporated a lot of elements from Warrior philosophies and the Asian martial arts into my system. You can also examine the example of the first-degree initiation later in this book to see how I've taken these Wiccan roots and modified them to suit my circumstances. The Warrior Initiation in the appendix (page 131), is a good example of patterns I developed outside the traditional Wiccan rituals.

The Wiccan Warrior can use any kind of mythology in his practice: Egyptian, Roman, Yoruban, you name it. Every religion on the face of this earth is based on mythology of some sort or other. Try saying that to a fundamentalist and see what happens! But it's true. The Bible is full of ancient myths. Many borrowed from earlier mythological systems. Myth is powerful because it presents us with metaphors and images that speak directly to our subconscious. The language of the subconscious is images. The ancient Biblical prophets knew this, because they used a device called "parables" to teach others. These little stories carried a verbal message for the conscious mind and a symbolic message for the subconscious. This is powerful stuff. But the moment that you start looking at myth as literally true, as the fundamentalists do, you negate its power.

A Wiccan Warrior doesn't wish for a "Golden Age" sometime in the distant past, or sit about endlessly dreaming of an unattainable future. The time for action is now. Paradise is available to you here and now, you just have to have the will to reach for it. For the Wiccan Warrior, there are no ordinary moments. If you want to live as they did in some mythical "Golden Age," do it! A Wiccan Warrior creates his or her own reality. What kind of reality have the Wiccans of the world created? In the next chapter we'll examine this reality and how it affects the Wiccan Warrior.

Endnotes

1. Jung, Carl. (1964) *Man and His Symbols.* Dell Publishing, New York, NY.

2. Musashi, Miyamoto. (1988) *The Book of Five Rings.* Bantam Books, New York, NY, p. 90.

3. From a presentation given by Sun Bear in California in 1985.

4. Sun Tzu, trans., Thomas Cleary. (1991) *The Art of War.* Shambhala, Boston, MA, p. 48.

5. Ibid., p. 35.

6. Piggot, Stuart. (1975) *The Druids.* Thames & Hudson, New York, NY, p. 11.

7. Slater, Kate. (1993) "White Horse Hill," "Songs of the Dayshift Foreman" newsletter, No. 55, Yule 1993.

8. Lady Sheba. *The Witches' Workbook.* p. 83.

9. De Givry, Grillot. *Witchcraft, Magic and Alchemy.* p. 109.

10. Farrar, Stewart. *Eight Sabbats for Witches.* p. 91. This is a slightly altered version of the fifth verse of Kipling's poem "A Tree Song" from the story of Weyland's Sword in *Puck of Pook's Hill.*

5

THE RATIONAL WARRIOR
Avoiding Fundamentalism

Men should be judged, not by their tint of skin,
The Gods they serve, the Vintage that they drink,
Nor by the way they fight, or love, or sin,
But by the quality of thought they think.[1]

—Laurence Hope

ANY SAFETY-CONSCIOUS cop will tell you that one of the most important safety principles is the elimination of habits and routine.
Keep going to the same coffee shop every shift at the same time, and
sooner or later somebody who wants to get you will figure this out, and
ambush you. A Warrior has no routines. A Warrior is, as don Juan so
aptly put it, "unavailable." The Warrior is spontaneous, fluid, and not at
all a creature of habit.

This does not mean that routines and regimens don't have their
place. But the Wiccan Warrior is not fettered by them; they shouldn't
prevent flexibility and innovation. They shouldn't be a liability. If a
change is called for, the Wiccan Warrior doesn't hesitate to change.
Bruce Lee put it this way, "Set patterns, incapable of adaptability, of pli-
ability, only offer a better cage. Truth is outside of all patterns."[2]

I first became involved in Wicca because I wanted such a change. I wanted an alternative to the dogma of mainstream religions. To my surprise, I found a lot of the same dogma in the Pagan community. The source of much of it is so simple, so insidious, that many fail to recognize it, or at least the full extent of it.

Most of us are first-generation Wiccans. We were brought up in a Judeo-Christian society and thoroughly indoctrinated in its thought patterns as children. Our views about the structure and function of religions and the universe are strongly influenced by this indoctrination. It was the Jesuit Ignatius Loyola who said, "Give me your children to train until they're seven years old." After that you could do what you wanted with them. The pattern is set, the die cast.

What seems to happen first is that Pagan individuals try to set up religious organizations recognized by state and federal authorities. There are many motivations for this, not the least of which is recognition from the public, government, and other institutionalized religions. This process in itself is the cause of part of the problem, because the rules for incorporating religious institutions in our Western society were written by members of the majority religion in the West: Christianity. They were written using its jargon and terms, and written to accommodate systems that were organized and structured as they were. Such rules may force covens to adopt permanent addresses, adopt the structure of a Christian church, assign officers in the organization Christian titles such as "minister," "pastor," or "bishop," and to call their organizations "churches" or "parishes." Suddenly we have an exclusive clergy, a hierarchy. In our zeal to become "respectable" in the eyes of society, we have often become more Christian than Pagan as we cloak ourselves with the trappings of "the Church."

If you've never looked into the etymology of some Christian titles that organized Wiccan clergy are now adopting, then check out the following examples:

Church: This word literally means "house of the Lord." It derives from the Greek root "kurios," meaning "lord, master." From this we get the adjective "kuriakos," whose use in the phrase "house of the Lord" later developed it into the noun, "kurikon." In medieval Greek this was contracted to "kurkon," brought into German as "kirche" and then into English as "church." The archaic term for a church in Scotland is "kirk," which comes from the same root.

Pastor: A Latin word, meaning "shepherd."

Bishop: This comes from the Greek word "episkopos," meaning "overseer." The Greek root words are "epi" ("around") and "skopein" ("look" or "observe"). It was used as a title for various government offices before being pressed into service to denote a church officer.

Referring to a Wiccan temple or coven by a patriarchal Christian term such as "church" is a curious custom in a religion that reveres a Goddess. Is "house of the Lord (i.e., Yahweh)" really the term that you'd want to use to describe your coven? Is the Priest or leader of your group really a "shepherd" or an "overseer?" If he is, does this make you part of a flock (of sheep)? If these terms don't precisely describe what you are doing, maybe you should give some careful thought to alternatives. Bruce Lee once pointed out that "the classical man is just a bundle of routine, ideas, and tradition. When he acts, he is translating every living moment in terms of the old . . . If you follow the classical pattern, you are understanding the routine, the tradition, the shadow—you are not understanding yourself."[3] Wiccan Warriors may borrow useful ideas from others, but they think for themselves. Only then can they achieve an understanding of self.

The Judeo-Christian-Islamic religions are all heirarchies; in other words, a group of clergy interprets religion for a congregation of lay followers. In Webster's dictionary, you'll find the following definition:

Hierarch, n. [LL. *hierarcha;* Gr. *heirarches,* a steward or keeper of sacred things; *hieros,* sacred, and *archos,* a ruler, from *archein,* to rule, lead.] one who rules or has authority in a religious group or society; a high priest.[4]

The clergy is believed to have established a special connection with deity. The clergy acts as intermediaries for their congregation, who don't have this special connection. Religion is dispensed. These religions often became, to one extent or other, religious businesses, devising different ways to make money to support these structures. Christianity became "Churchianity." Since such institutions often involve property such as a temple and administrative duties, there is inevitably a need for cash to maintain it. The larger the organization, the greater the structure required. The greater the structure, the greater the costs. Cash is also needed to feed the professional clergy required to administer the temple. Too often such organizations were created to enrich the bank account of the founder and serve his associates, not the congregation. Televangelists have turned religion into a lucrative business. Either way, this invariably leads to fund-raising schemes. How often do we see religious organizations running bingo games and casino nights to pay the bills involved? This is making money from the addictions of others. How ethical is this?

"Churchianity" became political. The Burning Times is an example of what can happen when such a state religion gains control over the minds of the people. Christians don't have a monopoly in this regard. Look at what the ancient Romans did to Christian martyrs in the coliseum. Clearly this sort of activity is contrary to the Wiccan Rede; people are being harmed.

And yet I've seen some Wiccan organizations mimicking all of the above behaviors. For example, if a coven decides to purchase land, or a permanent temple, it is committing itself to numerous overhead costs and responsibilities. Similarly, if a person turns their position as a Wiccan elder into a profession (i.e., their sole source of income) it puts an awful lot of pressure on them to make money by whatever means to provide the basic necessities of life for themselves. This pressure sometimes leads to questionable activities.

Many modern Pagan organizations that have adopted congregational models are quite benign and useful, but not all. The tendency of some modern Wiccan organizations to separate people into lay and clergy, secular and religious, is another example of dualism being superimposed on a monistic system. It is a curious thing that so many of us left traditional Judeo-Christian religious systems behind because of these activities, only to find some of our peers starting to model their Wiccan beliefs after it.

Now I am the first to recommend that we study other religions to obtain ideas that may be useful to the practice of our own. But dualism is not the way of the Wiccan Warrior. The Wiccan Warrior is a monist. She is an integral part of divinity. She does not need an intermediary between her and divinity.

The Judeo-Christian-Islamic families of religions are "revealed" religions. In other words, prophets or messiahs received the "word of God," usually through an intermediary like an angel. They then wrote their message down and distributed it to their followers, who made their own translations and interpretations of it. Then many of them sit about arguing, fighting (and often killing) over whose interpretation is correct. This literature is called "scripture," examples being the Torah, Bible, and Koran. For example, the prophet Mohammed went off into the wilderness and was visited by the angel Gabriel, who ordered him to record his recital. This is why the Islamic scripture is called the Koran. Koran means "recite."

The followers of revealed religions rely upon professional clergy to interpret and intercede with deities for them. Thus, these religions developed heirarchies, professional clergy leading lay followers. Lay people in a revealed religion access deity through their clergy.

I don't recognize prophets and messiahs. As a Wiccan Warrior, I have a personal connection with deity. This isn't some special gift. As Buddha and Jesus both pointed out, it is everyone's for the taking. In Wicca, every person has their own connection with deity. No one stands between me and the Gods. I don't need to have someone interpret religion for me. As a Warrior, I experience it directly, myself. You really don't need a Priestess or Priest to assist you. You can be a solitary practitioner. The great Samurai Warrior Miyamoto Musashi was never defeated. He taught himself.

Wiccans do not have books of scripture, such as the Bible or Koran, as revealed religions do. What we do have is a book listing our rituals and working notes called the "Book of Shadows." Many older books about Wicca will tell you that this name dates from the Inquisition. They'll tell you that it refers to the necessity of keeping the book secret, lest it gets you arrested by the officers of the Inquisition. This is a romantic story, but highly unlikely. Aidan Kelly reports:

> Valiente has suggested quite plausibly that Gardner may have gotten the term "Book of Shadows" from an article about an ancient Sanskrit manuscript that appeared in 1949 in *The Occult Observer*, a journal edited by Michael Houghton, the publisher of *High Magic's Aid*.[5]

Traditionally, a Book of Shadows is usually copied by hand from one Wiccan to the next. Originally many of them were handwritten in an obscure script, such as Theban, Malachim, Runes, or Over the River. I own two handwritten Books of Shadows and I wrote my first in Theban. I did this when I was young and caught up in the mystery and mystique of it all. After all, I believed then that this was top secret, ancient, arcane, occult knowledge. I know now that this was initially a practice more common in Occidental Ceremonial Magick. It was either intended originally as a simple security measure to prevent the book from being used by the uninitiated, or as a means of adding special power to the words. Since then I've discovered that it is a pretty good system for preventing me from reading my own Book of Shadows. Nowadays I write in my Book in plain English. Or to be more precise, in my journal in my personal computer.

A Wiccan Book of Shadows usually starts with a section called "The Ordains." Before C.E. 1250 the English word "ordeyen" meant "assign, decree, appoint, arrange." It can be traced back through Old French ("ordener") to a Latin root ("ordinaire") which means "to set in order." Thus the Ordains are, in fact, rules or bylaws for running a Wiccan coven. They are a collection of rules of order like the bylaws of a society or a sort of "Robert's Rules of Order" for Wiccans. The Gardnerian Book of Shadows includes 162 Craft Laws or "Ordains" (more or less). Some traditions of Wicca have shortened their list of Ordains from the traditional Gardnerian list.

Since the Ordains exist to assist in the administration of a particular coven organization, they need to be relevant to the needs of that coven. To be effective, they should be regularly examined. If it is found that they are no longer serving their original purpose, they ought to be modified or deleted, just like any functional society or organization does with its bylaws.

For instance, I pointed out the dubious necessity of maintaining the secrecy ordered by the thirteenth Ordain ("none but the Wicca may see our Mysteries . . .") earlier. Gerald Gardner "invented" these Ordains. They were not handed down from time immemorial as you may have been lead to believe. This being the case, blindly adhering to them as "gospel" seems foolish, at best. The Wiccan Warrior should carefully examine any doctrine or Book of Shadows presented to them. If it works for you, well and good. If not, the Wiccan Warrior adapts it to conform with the truth as known to them.

To the Wiccan Warrior, the Book of Shadows is a personal working journal in which he can record what works for him. All of the Books of Shadows that I've seen have included a collection of spells, chants, recipes, and rituals. But the Book of Shadows is not scripture. Wicca is not a revealed religion, remember? A Book of Shadows is more like a cookbook full of favorite recipes. No two Books of Shadows need be exactly alike. Although you have your grandmother's recipe for roast chicken, there are many other ways to cook a chicken.

Your Book of Shadows wasn't written by any prophet or messiah. You may have copied your initial Book from a version written by another member of your coven, who may have copied it from somebody else. But then you are just as free to add to it or modify it as Gardner did when he wrote "Ye Booke of Art Magical" and then rewrote it (several times) to create his first "Book of Shadows." I experience deity myself, in person. I'm my own prophet. I don't need intermediaries that try to tell me that their way is the only way. Others may share their experiences and show me the way that worked for them. But ultimately Wiccan Warriors discover the path for themselves.

The congregations of many Western religions are dwindling because they are not meeting the needs of their followers. Hence parishioners are leaving to seek divinity elsewhere. Institutions are dogmatically clinging to dysfunctional systems that were in use thousands of years ago. Religions must grow or they die. If we blindly mimic these outdated, ineffectual systems, we may share this fate. Change is a law of nature, remember? It isn't a good idea to copy a failing institution. This doesn't mean to say that such organizations don't have some useful things to teach us. We must take an objective look at them, taking what works for us and discarding the rest.

I doubt that most of the Wiccans that I see mimicking dogma borrowed from other beliefs are conscious of what they are doing. Children from dysfunctional families often grow up to start dysfunctional families of their own. This is equally true of members of dysfunctional religions. They tend to leave one harmful religion or cult only to join another equally destructive to their well-being.

This does not mean that patterns cannot be broken. This is exactly what being a Wiccan Warrior is all about. A person from a dysfunctional family can come to a realization of this dysfunctionality and break the cycle by making changes in themselves. But a person seeking to escape the influence of one religious group or destructive cult must be careful that they are not attracted to another group with the same characteristics and problems. Or even worse, that they create their own religious cult as destructive as the one they left. Familiar is not necessarily better. The world doesn't need any more fundamentalists of any description.

To start believing that there is one right path for everyone is to fall prey to exclusivity, the idea that there is only one true faith. It is an extension of the tribal mentality of religion: "These are the gods of my tribe and my tribe is the best, so my gods are better than your gods." It leads to evangelism, selling your religion to others as the only answer to everything. This simply isn't acceptable in today's world. Look at what is happening in the Middle East and in Northern Ireland. There are many valid paths to deity. We ought to be celebrating our similarities rather than nitpicking over our differences.

Wiccan Warriors think for themselves. They eliminate useless habits and routines. They are not fettered by dogma. They don't blindly mimic anyone. Wiccan Warriors have their own personal connection with deity. This is the source of their inspiration. These are the keys to their success.

Now that we've examined what it means to be a Warrior, let's move on and examine the tools and skills that the Wiccan Warrior uses to succeed.

Endnotes

1. Hope, Laurence (pseudonym for Nicholson, Adela Florence Cory, 1865-1904). "Men Should be Judged" from her collection of poems *Stars of the Desert*.

2. Lee, Bruce. (1975) *Tao of Jeet Kune Do*. Ohara Publications, Inc., Santa Clarita, CA, p. 15.

3. Ibid., pp. 16–17.

4. *Webster's New Twentieth Century Dictionary of the English Language*, Unabridged, Second Edition, ©1970, p. 858.

5. Kelly, Aidan. (1991) *Crafting the Art of Magic*. Llewellyn Publications, St. Paul, MN, p. 43.

Part Two

THE WARRIOR'S MAGICKAL ARSENAL

6

THE ENERGIZED WARRIOR

Using Energy

Creation in Hinduism depends on the five elements of ether, air, fire, water, earth. The first is ether, and ether is sound—the original sound, the nada. Out of the vibrations of nada comes the universe— it begins with sound, vibrations.

And sound is also used to conjure up a deity. In the beginning was the Word, the voice. When you are summoning a deity, you pronounce the seed syllable of the holy name.[1]

—Joseph Campbell

THE FIRST PRACTICAL thing that a Wiccan Warrior must do is learn how to raise and use energy. In his "20 Rules for the Dojo," Gichin Funakoshi, one of the founders of modern Karate, said, "Spirit first, technique second." So I'm going to start by discussing energy before I get into the details and techniques of magick.

A Wiccan Warrior trusts his personal power. As don Juan Matus puts it: "That's all one has in this whole mysterious world."[2] The Wiccan Warrior cannot separate the mental and magical process from the physical one. There is an old saying in Zen, "Ken-Zen Ichi Nyo" (Body and Mind, Together). Wiccan Warriors learn to become sensitive to the energy around them, and to connect with it. They use techniques to raise energy within themselves. The Wiccan Warrior then actively directs this energy with his will to cause change.

The concept of energy as a tool of the Warrior is common to many martial arts disciplines. In the Chinese and Japanese martial arts, this energy is known as *Ki* or *Chi*. Chi means "breath-energy" or "life-energy." Chi is directed by the intent of the practitioner. There is an old Zen adage, "Munen muso," which means, "Where there is no intention, there is no thought of moving." This tells us that the Warrior must use his will to move the Chi. Put another way, Chi follows the intent. You find this principle in many Asian martial arts. This is exactly what the Wiccan Warrior does in Circle: raising energy and directing it with the intent or will. The power in such martial arts techniques does not come from physical strength alone, "Something else moves the sword."[3] In Tai Chi Chuan a perfect punch is said to consist of ten percent strength and ninety percent Chi. Bruce Lee's one-inch punch, which we looked at earlier, is an example of this.

Preparation for Raising Energy

Since your body is the channel or valve through which the energy that you raise passes, it behooves you to keep it in good shape. As a Wiccan Warrior, I realize that physical fitness not only improves my magical ability, it is also good for my overall health and well-being.

Proper Diet

What you eat has profound effects on you. There is no point in working out if you're not eating right. A high-fat, processed diet or an excess of caffeine, tobacco, or alcohol can destroy more than your body. It interferes with your thought processes and causes changes in your energy levels. Anyone who has ever been in a Circle with someone who is drunk will know what I'm talking about here.

A balanced and healthy diet will stabilize your energy, clarify your mind, and improve your ability to conduct energy. Many say that a mostly vegetarian diet is the best for overall health and energy. The old adage to enjoy everything in moderation, but nothing to excess has been proven in recent studies to be true. The latest findings indicate that the addition of a little fish or poultry into a mostly vegetarian diet to be the healthiest. Adding a moderate amount of red wine or grape juice to the diet has also been found to be beneficial. Those of us who have been taking antioxidants for years are pleased to hear they've discovered that vitamins C and E and especially green tea to not only repel cancer, but to destroy it in the body. There are numerous benefits also from drinking at least eight glasses of fresh, clean water per day. All of these things that are beneficial to the body have an impact on one's spiritual or psychic fitness as well.

Diet can be used to deliberately bring on changes in states of consciousness. For example, fasting is a traditional means to bring on visions and trance states. When I was doing the solo practical phase of my Air Force survival training, I had extremely vivid dreams while I subsisted on the meager diet that I was able to glean from the forest. It was difficult to separate dreams from reality. When I went on to teach survival to cadets, I frequently observed this phenomenon among my students. Many seemed to be walking in a world between dream and waking. While fasting in a vision quest is certainly an effective technique, it is always best to do this under the supervision of another person who is not fasting. I know from experience that when you are fasting you tend to be weak and accident-prone. To survive in the wilderness, one needs one's wits about them, or at least someone to keep them out of trouble.

Of course, such trance states can also be achieved by using mind-altering substances. I avoid these. Drugs certainly do alter your consciousness, but they leave you with no control over the state that you find yourself in. Even worse, they can lead to debilitating and destructive addictions or brain damage. I consider alcohol a drug. There are those who argue that in some tribal cultures drugs were traditionally used to achieve altered states. While this is certainly true, it is also true that these cultures put those who used such substances through rigorous training to give the user control over such states. It was recognized by these cultures that not everyone could exercise the discipline to use these substances; even a small error in judgment could bring about disastrous consequences, even to an experienced person. With many street drugs and chemical hallucinogens, what is being touted as "altered realities" are merely the tricks your eyes play on you when your brain cells are being destroyed. There is no mystical import to chemically induced (and permanent) stupidity.

Since it is possible to achieve altered mental states without using such substances, using the techniques that I have described elsewhere in this book, I do not use drugs. In my opinion, the possible benefits are far outweighed by the risks involved. I have occasionally found myself in Circles where celebrants have showed up under the influence of alcohol or drugs. These individuals unbalanced the energy of the entire group, acting as an energy drain for the entire Circle. This is both inconsiderate and foolish.

Regular Exercise

Exercise helps to reduce stress that can sap your energetic reserves or block the flow of energy within you. Exercise can increase your capacity to handle psychic energy. It improves circulation of blood, lymph, and spinal fluid in the circulatory systems of the body. All three are essential to the well-being and effectiveness of your brain. Your body is a much better channel for energy if you are physically fit. Martial arts disciplines such as Tai Chi are especially useful to the Wiccan Warrior, since they are founded on the principle of improving the flow and use of energy, or Chi, in the body.

Physical exercise affects the Warrior in other ways as well. It teaches us the importance of balance, helping us to find our center. It fosters the discipline needed to strengthen one's will. It allows us to explore our limits and expand beyond them.

Adequate Rest

You can't do effective magick if you are fatigued. Fatigue makes concentration harder to achieve. If you are tired, be honest with yourself and get some rest rather than pushing yourself. Do your magick when you are fresh. Meditation is a useful tool; the mind rests in silence. If fatigue is a problem, check out the meditation exercises that follow in this book (see page 69).

Flexible Habits and Routines

I wrote previously that a Warrior was "unavailable." That is to say, a Warrior has no routines. She cultivates spontaneity and flexibility. A Warrior is free and fluid rather than predictable. A Warrior uses her knowledge of the habits and routines of his opponent to her advantage. At the same time, the Wiccan Warrior presents no patterns that the opponent can use.

This does not mean that a Warrior's life is random or disorganized. Nor does it mean that routines and regimens don't have any place in a Warrior's life. As a Warrior, I don't observe "Pagan standard time" (i.e., showing up for an appointment or somebody else's ritual whenever I feel like it). This is bad manners and bad karma. Having no routines simply means that the Wiccan Warrior is not a creature of habit. He eliminates routines and habits that serve no useful purpose and cultivates regimens that enhance his life.

Eliminating Obstacles

There are many misconceptions about obstacles to energy flow. For example, Gerald Gardner suggested that the reason witches should practice skyclad (that is, naked) is that clothing may impede the release of energy.[4] I've met many Wiccans who believe this. Yet one can find numerous examples of people who have practiced their telepathic and energetic skills through structures and across great distances. These same Wiccans will conduct a skyclad Circle in someone's house, raise energy, and direct it somewhere. Thus the energy that supposedly can't pass through their clothing is passed through the walls of a house, which are far more substantial. There may be other valid reasons for conducting a skyclad Circle, but this isn't one of them. Energy can easily pass through clothing.

In China there is a science of energy flow called *Feng Shui,* the ancient art of placement. People arrange their houses, their offices, and their furniture according to the rules of Feng Shui in order to optimize energy flow. I don't propose to enter into a lengthy description of the principles of Feng Shui here. Suffice it to say that the Wiccan Warrior must have their "earth altar" in order to raise and use energy effectively. The earth altar is your everyday, mundane world. If your house, your business, or your everyday activities are disorganized, then it's a pretty safe bet that your magick will be too. As a Wiccan Warrior, I try not to be haphazard about anything. The Warrior approach is applied to everything you do every day. A Warrior's environment is a reflection of the discipline that he practices.

Raising Energy Through Toning and Mantras

The word mantra comes from a Sanskrit root, which means to "think or reason." This is usually taken to mean verbalizing such thought. Any sound or combination of sounds could become a mantra. This is related to the ancient idea that knowing the correct name for a thing gives you power over it. This is a vital part of the concept of mantras: once you know the real name of a thing, you can create it by its sound.

This is the reasoning behind the ancient Hebrew prohibitions about speaking aloud the name of their God, usually rendered in Hebrew as YHVH, also known as the Tetragrammaton, a word which literally translates as "four-letter word." It was because of this prohibition that the Hebrews used corruptions of the pronunciation such as "Yahweh," which later became "Jehovah." There are myths all over the world concerning deities who got in trouble because their real name was somehow revealed or because they swore by their name and therefore couldn't evade their oath.

The German jazz historian Joachim Ernst-Berendt once enumerated the issue in three points: "(1) since the one sure thing we can say about fundamental matter is that it is vibrating and, (2) since all vibrations are theoretically sound, then (3) it is not unreasonable to suggest that the universe is music and should be perceived as such."[5] The magical power of song is a very old concept. A mythical example of this magickal power of words in song is in the epic Finnish poem, the *Kalevala*. In it, the god Vainamoinen transforms Joukahainen, who had angered him, into part of the landscape simply by singing.

In Tantra, there is a principle called "varna," which holds that sound is eternal and that every letter of the alphabet is a deity. Words become words of power. You can see something like this in Kabbalistic numerology systems which assign power to each letter of the Hebrew alphabet, although they don't take it quite this far. There is a parallel in the Norse Runes and their interpretations, too. This is also the basis of the ceremonial magician's grimoires. A grimoire is a list of words and names of power.

Related to this Tantric concept is the theory that every entity has a sound, which creates it out of the void, a "germ" sound (in the sense of germination). The Hindus call this germ sound "nada" and consider it to be the heart of creation. One example is the well-known mantra usually written as "OM," which is actually the triphthong "AUM." The "A" stands for "Agni," or fire, and is also related to the god Vishnu. "U" stands for "Varuna," or water, and is also related to Shiva. The "M" stands for "Marut," or air, and is related to Brahma. Thus, by chanting "AUM" you are invoking this trinity of deities.

In Eastern philosophy, mantras can take the form of single phrases, called "dharanis." Sometimes they are called "satya-vacana," which refers to the solemn uttering of a great truth. An example of using a dharani to invoke deities is the chant used by the Krishna Consciousness movement. It goes like this: "Hare Krishna, Hare Krishna, Krishna, Krishna, Hare Hare; Hare Rama, Hare Rama, Rama Rama, Hare, Hare." Hare means "Hail" and Krishna and Rama are deities in the Hindu pantheon.

Lest you think that this concept is foreign to Western culture, just look at the practices of the Christian church. Common mantras in Catholic churches include choruses of "Hallelujah," "Hail Mary," and the well-known phrase, "In the Name of the Father, and of the Son, and of the Holy Spirit." By saying these words, Catholics expect to invoke this power. But of course, as many a Catholic theologian will tell you, there is no magick in Catholicism!

In modern Wicca, chanting, toning, and song are modern terms for these old concepts of mantra and dharani. For example, in Gardnerian ritual there is a chant that goes, "I.O.EVO.HE. Blessed Be." Aidan Kelly points out:

> "Io Evohe" is based on the cry of the Bacchantes in Euripides' *The Bacchae*. Actually, I believe it is a multilingual pun based on "yod he vau he," the Tetragrammaton of the Kabala, since the Greek would other wise translate more exactly "as yo eh-oo-hoy." If the parting phrase of the Somerset witches, "A boy! Merry meet, merry part!" actually began with "Evohe," (quoting Margaret Murray) we must presume that their coven had been taken over by a renegade Elizabethan classicist, and that they are therefore not a trustworthy source for information about native English paganism.[6]

Toning is a modern variation of mantras that I use. In toning, a single syllable sound is repeated to raise energy. By using the proper mantras, the Wiccan Warrior can raise the type of energy needed and send it to where it is needed more effectively. Different mantras have different effects.

For example, try toning the well-known mantra "AUM" for a few minutes. Notice how it draws energy inward. Now try the mantra "MA" (pronounced as in grandMA). Notice how the energy is now flowing out from you. The first would obviously be most useful if you are trying to recharge your depleted energy at the end of a trying day. The latter would be more useful if you were trying to send healing energy to somebody else.

Another mantra that can energize you is the sound "HA." Take three sharp breaths in and then shout "HA!" Do this a few times and see how you feel. It is a very useful technique if you find your reserves depleted. The shout, or "kiai," that accompanies a punch or kick in martial arts such as Karate is actually this mantra. If uttered at the moment of contact, it helps to release the Chi. In Kendo, calls known as "katsu" are used with upward stabbing moves, and calls known as "totsu" with striking motions. Ever noticed how a weightlifter will yell while completing an especially heavy lift? It's the same principle at work.

A mantra that can relax you is simply the sound of a snore. Sit in a comfortable position, and make a soft snoring sound as you exhale (with practice you can make this sound while inhaling too). This will slow your breathing and heart-rate quite rapidly. A variation on this is called "Brummery breathing," in which you make a soft humming sound while you exhale. Part of the reason that this works is that it mimics snoring, a sound that you usually make when asleep. This triggers the same sort of relaxation response in your waking consciousness. This is a very useful technique the Wiccan Warrior can use to reduce stress.

Mantras are a particularly effective group technique. Get the group to stand or sit in a Circle, facing inward. Each person takes a deep breath and then utters the chosen tone until they run out of breath. They then quickly take another breath and repeat the tone. Because different people are running out of breath at different times, the sound of the group's mantra should be more or less continuous. Start with a low pitch. As each person feels the energy start to rise, they raise their voice an octave in pitch, or increase the volume. All watch the person directing the group. She or he will use some sort of agreed signal to indicate when the energy has peaked. In a group that is comfortable with each other, they will just know from experience. When the signal is given, all of the participants stop and direct the energy raised to wherever it is required. Alternatively, the participants, on seeing the signal, can direct the energy where it is needed, this having been agreed upon in advance.

Here is another group exercise that can be used by a coven to help one of its members by sending them healing energy, or helping them achieve some objective. For example, a person could use this if they needed extra energy for inspiration in finding a job. The person to whom the energy is being sent stands in the middle of a Circle formed by the other members of the coven. The members in the surrounding Circle may lift their arms to point their palms toward the person in the middle to help direct the energy. The group does toning, using an appropriate mantra. One effective technique is to use the name of the person in the middle of their Circle as the mantra. If they wish, they may alternate this with simple words representing the desire of this person. In the example given above, the words "success," "employment," or "abundance" would be appropriate. When the energy peaks, the participants stop toning and direct the energy to the person in the middle. They may actually touch the person if they wish. This is a very powerful experience for the person in the middle, surrounded by friends invoking him or her by name. It is particularly effective to improve a person's self image and confidence.

I've participated in many Circles where the group tried to raise energy by singing or chanting. But if you are working with a group of people who aren't very good at singing or who are self-conscious about their singing ability, toning can make it a lot easier for you.

Raising Energy with Dance

Remember that I wrote previously that Warriors *dance*? This isn't just a metaphor. Dance is another of the ancient ways of raising energy and working off stress. Anyone who has ever been in a dojo watching someone performing Karate *katas* ("forms"), or watched people in a park going through the flowing motions of the Yang Short form of Tai Chi, certainly cannot doubt that this is a form of dance.

Chanting or singing while dancing in a Circle has become one of the more popular ways of raising energy in Wiccan Circles. The songs used are brief, repetitive rhyming verses, a form of dharani. There are many such songs to choose from. One of the most popular is simply an invocation to the many aspects of the Goddess: "Isis, Astarte, Diana, Hecate, Demeter, Kali, Innana." Chants are often combined with dance. The dance should be relaxed and flowing. "The ultimate aim of dancing is to be able to move without thinking, to be danced."[7]

Dancing often includes the use of mudras or gestures. The Tantric term "mudra" (pronounced "moodra") is from a Sanskrit root meaning "to seal or close-off." A mudra is a gesture. Traditional Wiccan ritual is full of mudras. If you've seen someone tracing the pentagram in the air with their fingers or athame while calling the quarters of a Circle, you've seen a mudra. Mudras of this sort can be used at the completion of a dance to seal the magic worked and ground surplus energy before going on to other things.

One technique is to have the participants join hands and do a circular dance while chanting a particular mantra. As the energy increases, they go faster and chant louder. When the energy has peaked, the Priestess or Priest leading the dance will signal the participants by slowing to a halt and letting go of the hands of those on either side. The participants quickly turn inward and direct the energy thus raised to wherever it is to be sent.

A popular variation is the spiral dance, in which the leader of the dance leads the coven in a spiral inward. When the leader reaches the middle, he or she reverses direction, leading the group spiraling back out again. Thus, the group briefly has a double line of dancers passing in opposite directions. Once the energy peaks, the leader reforms the Circle and stops the dance, allowing the dancers to release the energy raised as in the previous example.

Raising Energy Through Drumming

The ecstatic use of the drum is not a part of mainstream religion in modern Western culture. Yet percussion is one of the world's oldest forms of music, and one of the most powerful ways to raise energy. War drums, like the Celtic bodhran, used to be very well known to the Warrior. Percussion instruments were the first and are among the most powerful musical instruments in our possession. "Percussion was almost universally used during such rituals of transition as birth, puberty, marriage, and death, when the spirit world is called upon for guidance."[8]

Anyone who has ever witnessed a performance by troupes of Japanese Taiko drummers like Za Ondekoza or Kodo cannot fail to have experienced the electrifying energy that they raise in each performance.

These troupes don't just drum, they *live* drumming. They live communally, eating pure foods, drumming and meditating as much as fifteen or sixteen hours a day. It is living a spiritual life with the central path to enlightenment being the drumming.

In fact, Za Odekoza ("Demon Drummers") is as good an example of a troupe of Warriors as you are likely to find. They were founded by Tagayasu Den on Sado Island in Japan in 1969. They prepared themselves through rigorous physical training in marathon running and the art of Taiko, the giant Japanese barrel drums. In 1975 they amazed the world by crossing the finish line of the Boston Marathon and immediately running to the stage to perform. Between 1990 and 1993, they performed in 355 U.S. cities, running from one city to the next between performances. One day they ran 64.64 kilometers. They wore out 121 pairs of shoes and averaged two dollars per day for meals, such was their dedication.

In India, apprentice drummers seclude themselves in huts for up to forty days in a retreat called a "Chilla." All they do while they are in the hut is drum. Within a few days they have all manner of visions. Shamans the world over "ride" the sound of their drums into other dimensions. Other religious traditions, such as Voudoun or Santeria, use drumming to summon spirits or gods down into someone other than the drummer, usually a dancer. In Voudoun, these spirits are known as "loa," and are said to be "riding" the dancers.

Drumming has an amazing effect on human consciousness. In 1665, Dutch scientist Christian Huygens discovered what is now known as "the law of entrainment." This law holds that if two rhythms are nearly the same and their sources are in close proximity, they will always tend to synchronize or "entrain." It is believed that this is because it takes less energy to synchronize than to pulse in opposition to one another. Psychologist Andrew Neher "found that he could 'drive' or 'entrain' the brainwaves of his experimental subjects down into what is called the alpha/theta border, meaning that a majority of the electrical activity in their brains was pulsing at a rate of between six and eight cycles per second."[9] The alpha/theta state is the state that occurs just outside the delta or sleep state, in which visions occur.

The Wiccan Warrior can recapture the motivational and meditation power of the drum known to our forebears. It's also an excellent way of lowering your stress levels. Any type of drum will suffice: a simple frame drum, djembe or dumbec, bongos, congas, you name it. For example, the Wiccan community in Denver holds regular "drum frenzies" that involve literally hundreds of people, many of them drumming and the rest of them dancing. Offshoots of this are covens formed strictly for ritual drumming without voice or words, just using the poetry of the drum to speak to the gods. It's a powerful experience.

Grounding Yourself

After you have been doing energetic work or magick, it is possible to build up surplus energy in yourself. This often makes a person feel lightheaded, dizzy, or unfocussed. Experienced Wiccans usually don't have this problem, because they have learned to use themselves as a channel or conductor of the energy, letting it all pass through without collecting or impeding it. However, everybody has "off" days when they don't feel 100 percent, and even an experienced person can have this surplus build-up of energy occur.

Several things are built into Wiccan ritual to allow the participants to ground excess energy. One is the ceremony of cakes and wine at the end of most rituals. Consuming food and beverages grounds out energy and returns a person to normal waking consciousness. Note: I don't use wine. I use nonalcoholic beverages like fruit juice. Alcohol is a drug (a depressant) that alters the mind. It does ground the energy, but I've seen far too many people use it too liberally and end up literally grounded (that is, flat on their faces). It also grounds the energy of the other people in the Circle. I restrict alcohol use to activities outside of the Circle.

Some covens have everyone place their hands on the ground or imagine that they are putting down roots. The participants imagine the surplus energy returning to the earth from which it came through these imaginary roots. One technique used by a coven I used to belong to was to have everyone grab hold of a staff held upright on the ground in the center of the Circle. We all imagined the extra energy running from us into the staff and then into the ground.

There are many variations on these grounding techniques that the Wiccan Warrior can use. One of my favorites is going out and working in the garden. I find that touching the soil naturally "grounds out" my surplus energy and restores my balance.

Raising energy is the first step. The next step is using your will to direct it. Now that we've seen how the Wiccan Warrior raises energy, let's take the next logical step and see how Wiccan Warriors prepare their minds so that they can more effectively use their will to direct energy.

Endnotes

1. Hart, Mickey. (1991) *Planet Drum.* HarperCollins, San Francisco. p. 17.

2. Castaneda, Carlos. *Journey to Ixtlan.* p. 167.

3. Musashi, Miyamoto. (1988) *The Book of Five Rings.* Bantam Books, New York, NY. Introduction, p. xxvii.

4. Gardner, Gerald. (1974) *Witchcraft Today.* The Citadel Press, Secaucus, NJ. p. 20.

5. Hart, Mickey. *Drumming at the Edge of Magic.* p. 119.

6. Kelly, Aidan. *Crafting the Art of Magic.* p. 100. Portion quoted from Murray, Margaret, *The Witch Cult in Western Europe.* p. 167.

7. Blacking, John. (1973) *How Musical is Man?* University of Washington Press, Seattle, WA.

8. Hart., p. 112.

9. Ibid., p. 114.

7

THE DREAMING WARRIOR

A Vision Quest

All men dream: but not equally. Those who dream by night in the dusty recesses of their minds wake in the day to find that it was vanity: but the dreamers of the day are dangerous men, for they may act their dream with open eyes, to make it possible.[1]

—T. E. Lawrence

THE ENERGY-RAISING techniques we have discussed so far are all means of changing one's consciousness. In other words, of achieving trance states. In this day and age the word "trance" has often taken on the connotation of being an unusual and unhealthy state. But this is not so. A trance is simply an altered state of consciousness. Entering altered states, or what Castaneda called "a separate reality," is what Wicca is all about. As we say in Circle, "A time that is not a time, a place that is not a place."

We alter our consciousness all the time. Do you remember being absorbed in a task to the point that you lost track of time? Or dancing all night to a local band when you were a teenager, not even feeling the least bit tired when you were through? If you do, then you've experienced forms of trances.

Changes in consciousness are what magick is all about. You can find examples of it in the Christian church. Catholics all practice a rite of communion that involves what they call "transubstantiation." Simply put, this is where the priest tells the worshipers that the wafers and wine have become the body and the blood of Christ. This, of course, involves a change of consciousness by the worshipers. Protestant denominations that use this rite call it consubstantiation, but it is, in essence, the same thing. It's magick, although some people would be loath to admit it.

There are two traditional ways to achieve a trance. In many tribal societies, the most common way is to use loud music, usually involving drumming, and vigorous dancing. This activity overstimulates the mind, causing a shift in consciousness. This is the method used in religions such as Voudoun and Santeria, for example. The other way, more common in Eastern philosophies such as Zen Buddhism or Yoga, is to use solitary contemplation or meditation, called samadhi. This meditation allows your senses to gradually shut down until everything, including your ego, fades away, bringing you into an ecstatic state known as satori. Satori is a state of pure and perfect awareness, unclouded by conscious thought. Both techniques require concentration; the first one on the external rhythmic stimulus being used, and the second on internal rhythms, like breathing.

Did you ever go for a long run or walk, and suddenly become aware that you didn't remember having any thoughts for the last kilometer or so? It's simply a sign that your mind has spontaneously entered a meditative state. Instead of getting shut down with one thought after another, you simply became aware of the present: Satori in motion. This sort of meditation in action is what is known in Zen as "chop wood, carry water." Once you've achieved some proficiency with the stationary exercises later in this chapter, you can try doing them while you're out for a jog, walking, or swimming. Eventually you'll be able to induce this state whenever you need it.

Canvass any group of police officers and you will find more than a few that will tell you that they rely on their instincts. Although few can probably explain exactly how they use their intuitions, you will be told numerous anecdotes of situations in which they heeded a "hunch" that ultimately paid off. What is happening here is that a set of circumstances causes them to spontaneously enter an enhanced state of consciousness, if only briefly. A Wiccan Warrior works hard to nurture this ability. Beat cops get nicknames, and on the beat I was known as "the Wizard," since more than one person has noticed my knack for finding persons and things that nobody else seems able to locate. All I am doing is enhancing my awareness, becoming aware of the subtle energies and currents around me: Satori in motion. I pay attention to what many people would probably dismiss, if they sensed it at all.

A martial artist is trained to cultivate this skill. Pure awareness is a very useful state of awareness for the Warrior. He lets go and becomes spontaneous action; energy follows intent. It is an equally important state for the Wiccan. In this state one can sense the subtle interconnecting currents of energy that surround us. With a mind clear of superfluous thoughts, we can more effectively focus our energy with our magickal intent.

I must emphasize that you are not "zoning out" and becoming oblivious to your environment with these exercises. What you are trying to do is *enhance* your awareness. You banish superfluous thought and achieve total awareness. Satori is a state in which all of your senses become fully functional. This is exactly what the Wiccan Warrior needs to become more effective. The following are a few meditative exercises that the novice can use to help develop their awareness.

Concentration and Breathing Exercises

Anyone can meditate, anywhere. The word meditation conjures up visions of a monk sitting in lotus posture, hands in his lap, staring into nothingness. But many people in Western culture find this posture uncomfortable. They are not as accustomed to sitting on mats or on the ground as people in some other cultures who practice this every day. Fortunately one can meditate just as effectively sitting in a chair. But certain elements are essential.

Upright posture is very important. It improves both breathing and the flow of energy or Chi. Sitting slumped over decreases the flow of oxygen and can eventually lead to distracting discomfort. One way to straighten your posture is to imagine a string attached to the top of your head. Imagine this string pulling upward, pulling your head and spinal column into line. This visualization will naturally put you into the best posture.

Some people find it useful to pick a spot to focus on, especially in the beginning. This may be a spot on the wall, a candle flame, or an arbitrary spot on the ground about six feet in front of you. A variation is to close your eyes and visualize an object like a feather or a candle flame directly in front of your nose. The trick is to breathe gently enough that your breath does not cause the imaginary feather or candle flame to flutter. Another trick is to imagine a vapor cloud coming out of your nose when you exhale, something like the cloud of vapor you see on a frosty day. When you inhale, the cloud is drawn back into your nostrils. You simply "watch" the cloud expand and contract.

Focus on your breathing. Let your stomach relax, and breathe deeply. Take a deep breath in, hold it a moment, inhale a little more, then exhale completely. Once you have exhaled, hold a moment, then exhale a little more before taking the next breath. You have to think about this process at first, but it very quickly becomes something you will do naturally without thinking about it. Inhaling a little extra before exhaling and exhaling a bit before inhaling helps you to do this deep breathing with less discomfort. After a few minutes your respiratory rate will naturally decrease as you relax.

Clear your mind of thoughts. The mistake that some people seem to make is that they try to force this process. The more they try to concentrate, the harder it seems. Just relax. If a thought comes, just say "thinking" to yourself and let it go. "Later, when you become experienced, you will not try to stop your thinking. You will let it stop by itself. You will let it go. You will realize that nothing outside you causes you trouble or anguish or fear or guilt or doubt."[2]

Another technique that I find useful is a posture known in Tai Chi as "holding the ball." You stand with your feet parallel, approximately shoulder-width apart. The weight is slightly forward on the balls of your feet and your back is straight (the string-on-the-top-of-the-head exercise is useful here). Your stomach is relaxed. The tip of your tongue is held lightly against the roof of the mouth. You are looking straight ahead at eye-level. You raise your arms and hold them at shoulder-height in front of you as if you were holding a giant beach ball against your chest. You focus on your breathing, feeling the Chi push out against your hands as you inhale and recede again as you exhale. A variation is to hold the arms low, with your hands at about navel-level, as if you were holding the imaginary beach ball against your belly. It won't take long before you feel the energy coursing through you.

Meditation on Shadows

One very useful exercise for expanding your awareness is to look at shadows instead of light. Most people, when viewing a tree in sunlight, look at the pattern of light as reflected by the leaves. Instead, trying focusing on the shadows. After a while this technique will train your mind to look at things more completely, to look for the unexpected.

Group Meditation Exercises

Hypnosis is another form of a trance. It is simply a directed trance experience. A person or persons are assisted in achieving trance states by a person who acts as facilitator. This works because, even in a deep trance, a person can still hear the facilitator, even if it isn't on a conscious level.

Leading a guided meditation or trance is pretty straightforward, and if you are part of a group, it is quite easy to accomplish. Here are some tips for the facilitator to keep in mind:

1. Try to do your speaking in time with the breathing of the person that you are directing, preferably on the exhalation of their breath. If you are doing this for a group, this becomes more difficult. You will have to allow enough time for the breathing of the participants to synchronize.

2. Always have the participants turn inward from reality and then onward to whatever vision is to be experienced.

3. Try not to use negatives. In other words, avoid saying things like "don't." Rather than telling the subject what not to do, give positive directions. Tell them what they *can* do.

4. Never give a command when leading a trance. Use the words "may," "could," "if," or "might." Some people will naturally put up resistance to imperative words like "must" or "shall" and this may interfere with their concentration. If you notice that a person is resisting, work with it rather than against it.

5. As in magick, visualization is crucial. Don't restrict this to the sense of sight. Involve all of the senses. Get the participants to see where they are, to hear the sounds there, to feel the wind on their faces and in their hair, to smell the scents of the place being imagined.

6. Be careful what depth you take your subjects to. This can be a problem if you want them to make verbal responses, as in past-life regressions. If you take them too deep, they may not be able to respond, and they may not be able to remember. If you discover that your subject is too deep in the trance to respond, ask for finger signals. It is possible to have them come up to a higher level by having them visualize themselves ascending stairs or floating up to a higher level.

7. Be alert to physical cues in your subjects. Watch their breathing, eye movements, and skin color. These will give you an indication of what the subject is experiencing, and whether they are feeling fear or discomfort.

8. If the subject is in distress, *don't panic!* Don't lose your cool and try to bring them out quickly. If your subject is in distress, having encountered an alarming vision or entity in their vision, give them a tool to deal with it. Tell them that they have a magickal tool or the abilities to take care of the problem.

9. It often helps your subjects if you tell them that they will have a "clear and vivid recollection" of their experience.

10. If you are doing past-life regression work, don't tell the subject what to expect or direct them to any particular time period. Don't give the subject any preliminary cautions, this will just curb their imagination, which they will need for the experience. Tell them instead that you are in control of the situation and will ensure that nothing untoward happens.

Warriors may use any or all of these trance techniques to achieve self-realization. With practice, these techniques become easier to use. With daily meditation many aspects of your life will come into balance. Your blood pressure may stabilize. You will be better able to handle stress. You will sleep more peacefully. Your energy levels will increase, and your sexual activities will improve. All aspects of the physical, mental, and psychic realms will be functioning better for you. One of the most magickal side effects of certain types of meditation is vivid, wild, and florid dream states. Some say that the difference between life with and without mediation is that when meditating regularly, life is in color when it used to be in black and white.

I don't use anything like drugs to enter trance states. I don't use anything that will interfere with my purpose and my will. The purpose of the Warrior is to clear away all distractions and become pure awareness. In the midst of a Tai Chi or Karate form, a Warrior does not think about the movements she is making; she becomes the movements themselves. You can't achieve this if you mess up your awareness with mind-altering substances. The mind is the Warrior's greatest tool.

Through training and meditation the Wiccan Warrior learns to enhance their awareness and clear their mind of distractions that will impede the will or intent. They practice satori in motion. All that remains is to take the next logical step and make magick.

Endnotes

1. Lawrence, Thomas Edward. (1971) *Seven Pillars of Wisdom.* Penguin Books, Harmondsworth, England, p. 23.
2. Musashi, Miyamoto. (1988) *The Book of Five Rings.* Bantam Books, New York, NY, Introduction, p. xix.

8

THE MAGICKAL WARRIOR

Principles of Magick

[The key to magic is] a paradoxical key, simple but perverse. You must get it right before you tried the turn, or bring the house down.[1]

—Vazkor the sorcerer

PEOPLE OFTEN ASSOCIATE magick with Wicca, and with good reason. Part of being a Witch is learning how to raise energy and using that energy to do magick. You'll notice that I spell the word magick with a "k." I do this to distinguish it from "magic," the sleight-of-hand tricks used by entertainers. This chapter isn't about magic.

Pick up any book on Witchcraft or magick and you are likely to find a definition of magick. You will find many differing definitions, depending upon the book you have picked up. Here are some examples:

Magic is a joyous exceptional experience which leads to a sense of well-being.[2]
  —Sybil Leek

Magic is the science and art of causing change to occur in conformity with the will.[3]
  —Aleister Crowley

Magic is the science of the control of the secret forces of nature.[4]
  —S. L. Macgregor Mathers, Order of the Golden Dawn

Magic is a comprehensive knowledge of all nature.[5]
    —Francis Barrett

Magic is the art of affecting changes in consciousness at will.[6]
    —William Butler

The work of magic involves transformation, and the first transformation is the shift of perception.[7]
    —Marion Weinstein

Effective magick works like this: The Middle Self chooses a purpose in harmony with its True Will; it communicates this purpose to the Younger Self in a special way, at the same time raising power; the Younger Self 'boosts' the power and channels it to the Higher Self, along with a clear image of the goal; and the Higher Self uses the power to manifest the desired result. Middle Self experiences the result, and the circle is complete.[8]
    —Amber K

Magic: (1) A general term for arts, sciences, philosophies and technologies concerned with (a) understanding and using various altered states of consciousness within which it is possible to have access to and control over one's psychic talents, and (b) the uses and abuses of those psychic talents to change interior and/or exterior realities. (2) A science and an art comprising a system of concepts and methods for the build-up of human emotions, altering the electrochemical balance of the metabolism, using associational techniques and devices to concentrate and focus this emotional energy, thus modulating the energies broadcast by the human body, usually to affect other energy patterns whether animate or inanimate, but occasionally to affect the personal energy pattern. (3) A collection of rule-of-thumb techniques designed to get one's psychic talents to do more or less what one wants, more often than not, one hopes. It should be obvious that these are thaumaturgical definitions.[9]
    —Isaac Bonewits

Each of these people has their own take on what magick is. As a result, they have methods that work best for them. Just as there isn't one right religion, there isn't one correct way to do magick. The Wiccan Warrior should use the system that works for him or her.

I don't think I've ever seen a book on Wicca that didn't include a section on magick of some sort. Examining the Wiccan books I've collected over the years, I have noticed that most contain magickal spells and rituals of a thaumaturgical nature. In other words, for practical, nonreligious purposes. A few contain theurgical magick; magick for religious or psychotherapeutic purposes. But not many go very deeply into the basics and history of magick. So before I go into the basics of how I practice magick, it will be useful to examine some of the history and philosophy behind it.

The English word *magick* first appeared in Chaucer's *House of Fame* (circa 1380). In Chaucer's work it was spelled "magik." In this form it meant the same as the Wiccan word "magick." So in effect, I am returning to an earlier spelling and meaning by spelling it this way. It can be traced back through Old French ("magique") to Latin ("magice") and ultimately to Greek ("magikos"). In its original Greek usage it referred to the arts of the Magi.[10]

Who were the Magi? The words Magi, Mage, and Magus come from the same source. "Mage" first appeared in the English language before C.E. 1350. About C.E. 1200, a "magy" was a person skilled in magick and astrology in the *Ormulum*. It can be traced back through the Latin "magus" and its plural "magi" to the Greek word "magos," meaning one of the Magi, or Magians, members of the Medean tribe (in what is now Iran), who were considered enchanters. Legend holds that members of the Persian priestly caste, in charge of rites, dream interpretation and so on, were members of this tribe. There is a reference to an enchanter of this tribe named "Simon Magus" in Acts 7: 9–24, in the Bible.[11]

In many of the earliest mythologies the deity that creates the Earth and everything on it is female. The Goddess/Creatrix literally gives birth to the Earth and its creatures. Patriarchal systems rewrote this, making the male deity the creator. Because in nature the male does not give birth, they had to come up with some different way for their god to create. You see some interesting examples of this in later Greek myths, such as Zeus giving birth to his children out of his head or thigh. In Judaism and Christianity, Jehovah begat the universe by uttering specific words. For example, in Genesis 1:3-6, Jehovah says, "And God said, 'Let there be light. . . . Let there be a firmament in the midst of the waters, and let it separate the waters from the waters' . . ."

This is similar to what is found in Chaldean magick, in which words are the tools used in magick. It subsequently became the foundation for a system I'll call Occidental Ceremonial Magick, which in turn is the basis for the ideas of magick most often presented in the modern popular press and in Hollywood horror movies.

Advocates of Occidental Ceremonial Magick believe that specific, appropriate words of power and form of ritual are critical to its success. In other words, to create, they need to use the same process used by Jehovah. The ritual must be performed precisely, without variation. This is another idea borrowed from Chaldean magick. The Chaldean magicians believed that random words had no effect, developing specific formulae for each spirit invocation and ceremonial occasion. Occidental Ceremonial Magick is full of incantations in which specific words must be said in a specific order, in which spelling and pronunciation is critical, and in which letters are assigned specific numerical values which give the words that they form specific mystical meanings. In fact, this is where we get the expression "magick spell" from. It comes from the Old English word "spell," meaning a saying, a tale, or a charm.

The idea of learning the proper name for things is an extremely old one. Phoenix McFarland explains:

> The ancient Finns believed that if you knew the secret name for a thing, then you could control the thing. The ancient Finns used the phrase "words of power" frequently. Finns believed in a whole pantheon of spirits and deities which could be controlled by magic and the magic was in knowing its name. The Finns also believed in the taboo against uttering the name of a totem animal aloud for fear of needlessly invoking it. So, speaking of a bear, a Finn says "The little brother in the warm coat." Baltic peoples say "Beautiful honey-paw, Broadfoot or Grandfather." Ural-Altaic peoples of Siberia call him "Little old man, Grandfather, Dear Uncle or Wise One." The Tete de Boule Indians in Quebec also call the bear

"Grandfather." In Sumatra, the tiger is called "He with the striped coat." In Java, the crocodile is called "Old One." To the Bechuanas the lion is called "Boy with a beard." To the Kols, the elephant is known as "You, with the teeth."[12]

Occidental Ceremonial Magicians control external entities and forces by either asking or compelling them to do their bidding. There are two processes used:

1. *Evocation:* Derived from the Latin root evocare ("to call out or forth"). Thus evocation is the process of calling forth and impelling outside entities to assist the magician. Evocation is used when the magician wishes to call upon malevolent powers. This takes the form of forcing or threatening demons to assist the magician, often by threatening divine retribution by the angelic "allies" of the magician.

2. *Invocation:* This word can be traced back to the Latin term invocatus, from in ("in" or "on") and vocare ("to call"). Thus the term invocation means "to call down" or "to call in." Invocation is the process of calling upon external entities to assist the magician. This takes the form of asking higher (benevolent) powers, such as Jehovah or his angels, to assist the magician.

As a logical extension of this, the devotee of Occidental Ceremonial Magick uses texts known as "grimoires." Grimoires are basically collections of magickal customs, recipe books of magickal spells, and directories of names and ranks of various entities that the magician may call, along with the signatures or "sigils" of these entities. Typically these entities are called angels and demons, though many other names and titles are also used.

Some entities found listed in these old grimoires were originally members of the Hebrew Elohim, an ancient Hebrew term for a fusion of all the gods. YHVH, or Jehovah, was originally simply one of the Elohim, a tribal god of Israel. Examples are Raphael, Gabriel, and Michael. The Hebrew suffix "el" means "god." So most of these magickal names are just synonyms for the Judeo-Christian God. Some that ended up being Christian "demons" were originally older Middle Eastern gods, such as Baal and Astaroth. Others are made up from the first letters of certain verses of the Bible. Many names found in such grimoires are corrupted or misspelled, reflecting the incomplete or incorrect grasp of Hebrew of the grimoire's author. Some, such as found in the Enochian system of the Elizabethan magician John Dee, were names "channelled" by Dee's medium, Edward Kelley.

In many books on magick there is a great emphasis put on the correct time to carry out a particular magical operation. This probably originates in Electional Astrology; that is, astrology used to determine the most auspicious time for a particular purpose. For example, *The Greater Key of Solomon,* and the *True Book of Black Magic* insist that magickal operations should be conducted only during specific hours and days ruled by the spirits and angels appropriate to the objective of the magickal work in question. These grimoires include elaborate tables and lists for calculating the correct and auspicious times for magickal work.

As centuries passed, many different philosophies influenced the practice of Occidental Ceremonial Magick. One important influence was the Kabbalah. This system, developed in the Middle Ages, describes how things come into manifestation from the Godhead through a series of stages called Sephiroth. Other mystical arts which influenced Occidental Ceremonial Magick include Gematria, Geomancy, and Tarot. To this was later added the unique Enochian system of magick and language created by John Dee in Elizabethan England. Alchemy and folk medicine were often included. This is where Shakespeare got the idea to have his three weird sisters concocting a brew in a cauldron in *Macbeth.*

Some disciples of Occidental Ceremonial Magick became solitary practitioners, while others have formed lodges and fraternities to practice as a group. Examples of such lodges are the Astrum Argentium, the Rosicrucians, the Hermetic Order of the Golden Dawn, the Fellowship of Isis, and the Ordo Templi Orientis. Contrary to popular belief, modern Satanists have drawn much of what they understand magick to be from this primarily Christian Occidental tradition, rather than the reverse.

Occidental Ceremonial Magick involves the use of elaborately decorated temple rooms or circles, ornate costumes, and numerous ritual tools and props. The costumes, tools, and props vary depending upon the purpose of the ritual they are to be used in. The rituals are performed in an ornate magick Circle drawn upon the ground or floor. This Circle is meant to serve as a protection for the magician; it keeps the entities and forces of the universe called upon by the magician outside. The magician calls demons, angels, and other entities into a designated area outside of the Circle, usually a triangle. The basic idea was that Jehovah and company were all right to have inside the Circle, but it was better to leave Satan and the bad guys outside. Not all groups follow this pattern however. For example, the Temple of Set, an offshoot of Anton LaVey's Church of Satan, considers protective Circles to be unnecessary.

Now let's go back to the beginning and the other genesis myth, the Goddess giving birth. Words and ceremony are irrelevant in this nativity. It is essentially a very simple and natural internal process. Using this model, magick becomes a simple matter of raising energy and directing it with your will, giving birth to magick.

Both systems require the raising of energy. Both require the development of one's will and visualization in order to direct it. But giving birth to magick is, in my view, a much simpler system. Most cops are familiar with the KISS principle (Keep It Simple and Straightforward). The fewer things that you need to worry about, the less that can go wrong. This principle applies equally well to magick.

A Wiccan Warrior recognizes that they are an integral and inseparable part of the system. We are linked to everything around us, energy permeating everything. The Wiccan Warrior senses this energy, draws upon it, and directs it. What is of primary importance is our ability to visualize what we wish to accomplish. It is the will that directs the energy or Chi. This is a process that does not necessarily involve words, costumes, paraphernalia, and elaborate rituals.

This is another place where the KISS principle comes in handy. People get all caught up in the idea that in order to practice Wicca or magick, one needs all kinds of magickal tools, clothing, and equipment. This is absolutely untrue. It is *you* giving birth to the magick, not your athame. If you think that you can't cast a Circle, raise energy, or practice magick without tools such as altars, the athame, and robes, then you're fooling yourself. Such tools can assist you, especially if you are just starting out. These tools and props act as focal points; subtle cues and symbols to help you accomplish your purpose. They are also helpful in large or public rituals, for the same reasons. But the Wiccan Warrior should always be striving to get used to working without them, because the real source of magick is *you*. This is one of the reasons that I was critical of that "crystal warrior autoelectromag" thing mentioned in the first chapter. The Wiccan Warrior doesn't need gimmicks to succeed.

Some Wiccans clutter their Books of Shadows with Occidental Ceremonial Magick, names and sigils from Medieval grimoires and Hebrew magical procedures, preserving fragments of a system without understanding what it is really all about. We saw earlier in this book how some spells and invocations found in the Gardnerian Book of Shadows can be traced to medieval grimoires, principally the *Greater Key of Solomon*. Most of these grimoires are of no use to the Wiccan Warrior. As Bonewits writes, "Except to the literary analyst and the thaumaturgical theorist, they are totally useless."[13] Most of the currently available grimoires have survived from the Middle Ages. Examples of such books are the *Greater Key of Solomon*, the *Lemegeton* or *Lesser Key of Solomon*, *The Sacred Writings of Abremalin the Mage*, and *The Grimoire of Honorius*. The authors of nearly all of them claim them to be much older than they really are (here is that fallacious "older is better" theory again). The authors of many of them claim them to have been long lost books written by famous persons such as King Solomon, which they most certainly were not. In other words, some of them were obviously written by ancient snake oil salesmen for a gullible audience.

One modern grimoire is a perfect example of this nonsense, the *Necronomicon*. It looks pretty much like the grimoires already mentioned. I am continually running into people (both Wiccan and Christian) that think it is an actual (ancient) magickal text. The truth is that it is a clever hoax.

The well-known fantasy writer H. P. Lovecraft mentioned the *Necronomicon of Abdul Alhazred* and several other imaginary grimoires in his novels. Lovecraft didn't write any of these fictional magickal texts. He simply invented the title and created a few "quotes" to use in his stories. In the mid-1970s, a shrewd promoter came up with the idea of having someone write a *Necronomicon* so that he could sell it to the uninformed. There are at least four versions of it, one of which simply repeats the first twenty pages repeatedly, as if the publisher expected that no one in his right mind would read any further before discarding it!

There is another very good reason why these old magickal procedures and spells aren't effective in today's world. Simply put, one of the principles of magick is that if one adds an emotional charge to it, the magick will work much better (more on this later). The problem is that the sort of things that invoked a particular emotion in the sixteenth century will not necessarily arouse the same emotions in the twentieth century. Culture, language, and customs have changed and our knowledge of how these things work has expanded too.

For example, in the sixteenth century, common expressions such as "God Damn It!" or "Jesus Christ!" were very emotionally charged expressions. They were shocking profanities that would at the very least raise a few eyebrows. Today they aren't likely to draw any attention at all. It is possible to train yourself into the correct mindset to make the old systems work. If this is what works best for you, have at it. But it is very likely that this mindset won't be applicable to other functions in your life. I have found that it is much easier *and* more effective to learn the principles of magick and apply them to create my own modern rituals, suitable for my own conditions. Remember that the Wiccan Warrior lives in the present. As Isaac Bonewits puts it, "If you can't think fluently in Hebrew, you have no business trying to do Kabbalistic magick."[14] I don't think in Hebrew, so I don't bother with Occidental Ceremonial Magick.

Attention to detail is important, but I believe that unnecessary detail makes one's magick less effective. The Wiccan Warrior makes a careful and objective inventory of their magick, identifies unnecessary practices, and eliminates them. Paring down your practice of magick to essential elements allows you to put more emphasis on those essentials.

"Power With" versus "Power Over"

Grimoires of Occidental Ceremonial Magick often require the magician to dominate someone or something through invocation or evocation. This is what modern Witches call "power over." In other words, one is invoking or evoking entities to have them do your will. As I pointed out earlier, many magicians invoke what they call "higher beings," since their perspective is that deity is on a higher level than we are and external to us. They evoke aspects of the self, nature spirits, and elementals, as if these were on lower levels. Magickal systems of this sort tend to keep forces external, working outside yourself.

This isn't the way of the Wiccan Warrior. The Warrior's power is "power with." The aim is to harmonize or entrain oneself with things, which all exist on one level, overlapping. There is nothing external; everything is interconnected. Wiccan Warriors are the valve, letting the energy or Chi work through them, in an internal process.

Another important aspect of this is the ethics involved. The Wiccan Warrior never does magick for another unless that person has specifically asked for it. A common example is the Wiccan who works healing magick for a terminally ill friend without asking this friend first if this is what they want. If this friend were dying and longing for release from pain, using magick without their knowledge to keep them here may be contrary to their wishes and cause them unnecessary suffering. A Wiccan Warrior remembers the Wiccan Rede at all times: Harm none.

Exercises to Eliminate Habits or Routines

In the last chapter I listed some exercises for raising energy. Once this energy is raised, the Wiccan uses his will to direct it to accomplish the purpose of the magick. The following are a few magickal exercises that Wiccan Warriors can use to help achieve their objectives.

Cord Magick I: Cord Cutting

One way to help you eliminate habits or detach yourself from persons or things that may be holding you back is *cord cutting*. You take a number of cords or strings, each representing an aspect or person involved. One end of each you tie to some object: it could be the altar, a tree, a candle stand, whatever. The other ends you hold in one hand. As you visualize these strings as representing the bonds holding you back, you take a knife or a pair of scissors and, one by one, cut the cords. This is a form of initiation (more on initiations later). It is a symbolic ceremony that helps your mind separate itself from whatever impedes it.

Exercises to Achieve Objectives

Cord Magick II: Braiding

Take three equal lengths of cord, side by side. At one end tie the three cords together. You can then secure this end to some sort of anchor, like a chair or table, or have another person hold this end while you work. The object of this form of magick is to visualize the successful accomplishment of your magickal goal while you braid (or knot) the cords.

With each new knot or braid, you think of another aspect of your objective. You can actually speak these thoughts aloud as you do each braid or knot, if you like. The longer the cords that you use, the more likely it is that you will either have to repeat yourself. You may have to think long and hard to think of additional things to visualize or voice aloud, and that is the secret behind this form of magick. It forces you to focus on what you are doing and constantly come up with new ideas about your objective, thus increasing your concentration on the task at hand.

Cord Magick III: Magickal Webs

This is a group exercise. Have the participants sit in a circle, facing inward. Take a piece of cord long enough to form a circle large enough that each of the coveners can hold it. Have them stretch it tight. Then take a number of other rolls or spools of cord and attach the ends at random points along the circumference of this cord circle.

Now have the coveners pass these rolls across the circle to one another, weaving them through the crisscrossing cords as they do so, forming a sort of web. If it's a big enough Circle, you can actually crawl under the web and weave your strands back and forth. As the web grows, have the participants visualize the sort of energy that they want to put in the web. They can verbally state these ideas as they visualize them. When all feel that they have woven enough energy into the web, tie off the free ends and cut off any extra cord on the spools. The web can be displayed or stored where it is needed.

Candle Magick

This is a very old technique. It is a variation on the meditation exercises described earlier. The candle serves as a tool helping the Warrior to focus his energy. The color of the candle may be chosen to represent the type of work to be done. This helps the Warrior to visualize the purpose of the magick. Anointing the candle with oil or writing upon it while concentrating on the purpose may be used to enhance this energy. Once the candles (and the mind of the Warrior) are charged, the candle can be left burning in some safe location where it does not present a fire hazard. You can then leave it to do its work. It doesn't matter that the candle may not be visible to you. Every time you think of the candle, it refocuses your will on the objective.

So now that we know how to raise energy and work magick, all that remains is to show you how the Wiccan Warrior uses these in ritual to achieve his objectives.

Endnotes

1. Lee, Tanith. *Vazkor, Son of Vazkor*, p. 204.

2. Leek, Sybil. (1971) *The Complete Art of Witchcraft*. Signet, New York, NY.

3. Crowley, Aleister. *Magick in Theory and Practice*. Castle Books, New York, NY, p. xii.

4. Amber K. (1990) *True Magick*. Llewellyn Publications, St. Paul, MN, p. 4.

5. Barrett, Francis. (1967) *The Magus*. University Books, Inc., New York, NY, p. 13.

6. Bonewits, Isaac. (1970) *Real Magic*. Creative Arts Book Company, Berkeley, CA, p. 28.

7. Weinstein, Marion. (1980) *Positive Self Magic: Occult Self Help*. Phoenix Publishing, Custer, WA, p. 9.

8. Ibid., p. 63.

9. Bonewits, p. 258.

10. Barnhart, Robert K., ed. (1988) *Barnhart Dictionary of Etymology*. H. W. Wilson Co., p. 622.

11. The Bible, Revised Standard Version.

12. McFarland, Phoenix. *The Power of Names*. p. 40.

13. Bonewits, p. 79.

14. Ibid., p. 257.

9

THE RITUAL WARRIOR
Revitalizing Ritual

And what have kings that privates have not too,
Save ceremony, save general ceremony?
And what art thou, thou idol ceremony?
What kind of god are thou, that suffer'st more
Of mortal griefs than do thy worshippers?
What are thy rents? what are thy comings-on?
O ceremony! show me but thy worth.[1]

—William Shakespeare

A LL OF LIFE is a ritual. Ritual is magick and energy in action. The word ritual comes from a Latin root related to numbering or counting the ways that a thing can be done. In other words, it refers to a series of events, one following another. Ritual is one of the tools that the Wiccan Warrior must master. Through ritual the Warrior can bring about change.

Forms of Ritual

In the previous chapters we've seen what kinds of odd elements ended up in some of the original Wiccan books of ritual. But simplifying or improving rituals isn't the only reason to write your own. Wiccans like me have always encouraged others to write their own rituals. As I said earlier, I believe that creativity and poetry are very much part of the Craft. Some traditions prefer a lot of ritual drama in their Circles, while others want to keep their Circles very simple. This is hard to achieve if you are relying on finding suitable rituals in books written by somebody else.

Rituals are most effective if they are designed to suit specific events and rites of passage. This being the case, a ritual written for a specific event is likely to be more effective than a "standard" ritual taken from some text. For example, initiations can be much more personal if specifically designed for the person they are intended for. Within a basic structure of elements, I like to improvise and customize each ritual. No two rituals are quite the same for me.

Some people may find this a bit disconcerting. Some people feel more comfortable doing the same rituals over and over again. Often these are general purpose rituals that somebody else wrote; they simply borrowed them out of a book. This may work for you, but this doesn't work for me. Books of other people's rituals may serve as a source of inspiration for my own, but I'm a Warrior and I like a challenge. I've taken charge of my life, why should I not take charge of my rituals, too?

A few years ago, I recall a group of "old guard" third-degree Wiccans who held a ritual designed for initiates only. This of course excluded a large number of people at the festival who were not initiated. Another Wicca Priestess, a true Warrior and teacher, put together a ritual to give the noninitiates something to do. The energy and enthusiasm in that ritual was truly phenomenal. It grew into something no one expected. Shy people were moved to get out into the Circle and dance ecstatically in public. In fact, so much energy was raised by these novices that several of the old guard sheepishly admitted later that they wished they had gone to the novice ritual instead. The "old guard" ritual had been very dull and predictable.

For me, one of the most important aspects of performing ritual is the aspect of spontaneity. If the muses, gods, or whatever else move you to do something different, I say go for it! For example, one place where spontaneity may be used is in the quarter invocations made at each of the cardinal points of the Circle (east, south, west, north, center) while casting. These invocations call upon deities, spirits, or ancestors to protect and guard the Circle. Sometimes, at the last minute, my wife and I have asked the people that we're circling with to use whatever words they are inspired to say as their quarter invocation. They usually don't know precisely what words they're going to use to call the quarters until they open their mouths to call them. They've been taught the elements and symbolism that relating to each quarter and apply it to suit the circumstances.

This can produce some amazing results! Sometimes we call the quarters by using songs, sometimes by using sounds that represent the elements at each quarter. For example, in the east we may use wind chimes that sound when we direct breezes at them with a fan. In the south we may use a drum, representative of sexual root chakra energy. In the west we may use an "ocean drum," a frame drum with tiny ball bearings in it, that when tilted gently back and forth makes the sound of waves. In the north, we may crack rocks together or use a gong to simulate thunder. In the center, we may use a Tibetan singing bowl, a brass bowl played by running a stick around its rim to create an eerie, ringing sound.

Words aren't important in this process. What is important is that the person calling the quarter (and better still, the whole coven) *visualizes* the energy and entities being called coming to guard and bless the Circle. Images are the language of the subconscious. The words, songs, or sounds that you use are simply tools to help you do this visualization.

For example, you may not relate to the symbols traditionally associated with the elements. A salamander may not conjure up images of fire for you. If this is the case, it might be better to draw from your own experiences when trying to visualize the elements. I'm a pilot who has flown everything from jet aircraft to hang gliders. The floating sensation of hang-gliding or the weightlessness briefly experienced in a zero-G maneuver definitely invokes images of air for me. The tumbling, roaring, spraying experience of a river raft on rapids might be a good image for water. Memories of blistering summer days in Arches National Monument in August or standing before a roaring Beltaine bonfire might be a good image of fire for you. Sitting in an echoing cave or wandering in an ancient rain forest might be the image you need for earth. Look back through your experiences and choose what works best for you.

I know that saying this may raise the hackles of some Wiccans who have been doing their Circle exactly the same way with no changes for decades. In answer to their concerns, I'd like to give you the following quotation from Isaac Bonewits:

> Due to the thousands of physical, psychological, psychic, and artistic variables involved in even the simplest use of a psychic talent, it should be remembered that no two rituals or their results are *ever* really "the same." Those who are obsessed with Repeatability in their research will find themselves repeatedly frustrated. Those who insist on performing written ceremonies word-for-word and gesture-for-gesture, without understanding the intellectual or artistic reasons for the original ritual designs, are also doomed to failure. In fact, a major problem of modern western occultism is that students are not taught to allow room in their rites for spontaneous changes and additions. This is a result of monotheistic theurgical attitudes ("there's only *one* way to do the ceremony"), white middle class biases ("only the ignorant or stupid lower classes have undignified rituals"), lack of experience with really intense energies, and traditional fears of unruly spirits, that is to say, the return of the repressed (something that terrifies intellectuals). But what good is a letter perfect ritual if it doesn't work very well (or at all)? . . . You can have both discipline *and* creative freedom—ask any good jazz musician, or dancer, or painter, or scientist.[2]

Some people get very upset when mistakes are made by themselves or others in a ritual. Lighten up! Intent is more important than form. If you make an error, let it go. The Warrior doesn't cloud his perceptions with useless emotions. This doesn't mean that a Warrior doesn't have any; it simply means that the Wiccan Warrior doesn't let them cloud her awareness. The way to control your emotions, then, is to let them flow and let them go.[3] To err is human. A Warrior may be striving for perfection, but everyone is bound to make some mistakes along the way. If you get hung up on thoughts of how you screwed up, you're not focusing on the task at hand. In combat this can be a fatal mistake. In ritual it's going to diminish, if not nullify, the results of the work you are doing. Besides, ritual should be an enjoyable and uplifting experience. As I say, if you aren't enjoying your religion, then you are either doing your religion wrong or doing the wrong religion.

There are many different types of rituals. Blacksun identified ten different varieties in his book *Three Times Around The Circle*:[4]

Social Rituals

1. Rituals of Salute

2. Rituals of Communication

3. Rituals of Status

4. Rituals of Interaction

Sacred Rituals

1. Rituals of Worship

2. Rituals of Celebration

3. Rituals of Passage

Specialized Rituals

1. Rituals of the Workplace

2. Rituals of Play

3. Rituals of Solitude

Murry Hope identified twelve different types of ritual in his book *The Psychology of Ritual*:[5]

1. Recollective ceremonies: The remnants of rites of earlier civilizations.

2. The worship or acknowledgment of cosmological or celestial influences.

3. Pantheistic, Pagan, and Animistic Rites (Seasonal rituals and Sympathetic Magick would come under this category).

4. Placatory or Propitiatory Rites.

5. Ancestral Rites.

6. Self-Exploratory Rites.

7. Fertility Rites.

8. Social Rites, including Birth Rites, Maturation or Puberty Rites, Last Rites, and Funeral Rites.

9. Sacrificial or Expiatory Rites.

10. Initiatory Rites, including Rites of Submission; often include physical mortification or deprivation.

11. Supplicatory Rites, including general unspecified collective prayer offerings and invocations which may or may not involve energy exchanges (gifts). May be purely devotional or may include specific pleas for bounty or assistance.

12. Rites of Protection, including Purification, Banishment, Cleansing, and Healing.

Most rites include a combination of the above categories. So you see that for every aspect of human existence you can create a ritual. It can touch every part of our being—a powerful tool for the Warrior indeed.

Don't be afraid to be spontaneous. Some of the most powerful rituals that I've ever participated in went off in a direction that was not intended. One of the most memorable occurred at Dragonfest in the Colorado Rockies. It was at a Circle attended by more than 300 people. It was a very powerful ritual drama commemorating the Salem witch hunts. The theme of the festival was "building community." The ritual consisted of a series of vignettes, beginning with the Goddess and God giving light to primitive peoples. The light was passed on from group to group, each group representing a different generation. The light was nearly extinguished at times, but eventually it made its way to a group representing the present age.

Now at this point what was apparently supposed to happen was some singing followed by a spiral dance. Everyone started singing:

Lady, Lady, listen to my heart song,
I will never forget you
I will never forsake you.

I was incredibly moved. I was in tears. I found myself staring at a person with whom I had a disagreement at another festival months earlier. She was staring right back. Suddenly we found ourselves crossing the Circle and taking each other in our arms. We apologized and sang that song to one another. Within seconds other people who had argued in the past, whose relationships had experienced difficulties, were crossing the Circle and making up. Everybody was standing in pairs or small groups singing to one another: "I will never forget you, I will never forsake you."

The organizers of the festival later tried to describe what had happened as resembling a "mass handfasting," though this doesn't even come close to describing the emotions involved. It still brings tears to my eyes years later. All because the Muse called and we let ourselves go with it.

Taking a Warrior Name

The first ritual step that the Wiccan Warrior takes is the taking of a magickal, or Craft, name. Taking a name for yourself like this may seem to be a simple and even trivial step. But names can have great transformative powers. They help shape our perception of what we are or what we intend to be. In many ancient societies people were first given a childhood name. When they became adults, they took an adult name. For example, the childhood name of the mythical Celtic Warrior hero Cuchulain was "Setanta." He didn't take the name "Cu ("hound") of Chulain" until he had demonstrated by his feats of skill that he was ready to become an adult. In *The Complete Book of Magical Names*, Phoenix McFarland put it this way:

The names we choose for ourselves can serve as magical tools as we travel on our individual paths. A name can be an inspiration (Venus, Athena, Phoenix); it can label us by our attributes (Quicksilver, Elder, Oak, Golden) . . . and can inspire us to change. Our names can associate us with elemental powers and bring that energy into our lives (Ariel, Sundance, Cascade, Terra). A name can help to improve how we feel about ourselves (Willendorf, Gaia, Balder, Plato). It can emphasize where we are now or where we hope to go. It can make us feel more powerful, wiser, more beautiful, more commanding, gentler, stronger, more female/male, more exotic, more innocent, more sexual, more enthusiastic, more fertile, etc. There is no limit to what a name can bring into our lives, except for those limits we put on it ourselves.[6]

The name that you choose for yourself may be a secret name, known only to you or only to a close circle of associates. This is a very old practice.

In many North American Indian cultures, it was believed that everyone and everything had a name that may remain hidden, which perfectly described one's innermost nature. The name might be revealed confidentially at some point, but the word had such sacredness to it that it was considered an extreme discourtesy to utter it aloud. . . . Secret names, known only to the owner, have to do with a belief in name–soul connection. In myths and folklore, the discovery of the secret name gives the discoverer power over the owner of the name. In many religions, the names of the Gods are the secret property of the priests. . . . Many cultures thought it was unlucky to reveal the name of a newborn to anyone outside the family before the child was christened.[7]

You may also choose to have a public pseudonym like mine now is. When I first stepped onto the Wiccan path, I was a shy, retiring, fifteen year old. Not a very imposing figure. I wanted to become stronger and more outgoing. I originally chose the Warrior name Conan as a magickal name. Subconsciously, I probably realized that this name was a symbol of what it was I wanted to become. Consciously, it simply appealed to me. My keeping it a secret name was not so much due to the observance of a magickal rule as it was due to embarrassment. I thought that anyone who found out my magickal name would laugh at me. This was because I hardly resembled the Warrior images it invoked to me at the time, not to mention all the macho-stereotyped nonsense that went with the comic book Conan persona familiar to many members of the public.

When I decided to take up antidefamation work ten years ago, I changed my Craft name to Kerr Cuhulain, another Warrior name. This name I use publicly. It defines who I am. I'm not concerned about what other people think about me anymore. I've gained the confidence and self-esteem I lacked as a youth. Choosing a name like I did helped me to focus the dream that I had originally and turn it into reality. When I was ready to begin a new phase, I chose another name to mark that transition. You can use your magical name as a tool for self trans-formation like I did. *The Complete Book of Magical Names* by Phoenix McFarland is an excellent resource for names and naming practices for those looking for a suitable magickal name.

Creating Your Own Rituals

Creativity and spontaneity are essential to successful ritual, but so is being organized. Using unusual special effects and gimmicks such as the ones that I've suggested can be effective, but only if it fits into an overall plan. You must be clear on the purpose or intent of your ritual before you start. Otherwise, it won't be effective. Energy has to be directed to achieve any magickal purpose. The Wiccan Warrior uses the principle of planning and preparation to help focus intent and facilitate action.

There are other reasons for thinking out your rituals beforehand, too. For instance, you can't use the same ritual techniques that you'd use for a coven of thirteen in a ritual that you intend to put on for 413. Ritual for large groups tends toward ritual drama; a performance rather than a participatory ritual. The more people participating, the more time it will take for them to carry out any individual act. The harder it is for the ritual leader(s) to give them cues to coordinate and choreo-graph the action.

For example, more than once I've seen people attempt to do the "cakes and wine" ceremony for groups of 300 or more. With a small coven, having people pass a single chalice and a platter around only takes a few minutes. But with a large group this takes so long that the momentum of the ritual is lost. People's concentration is broken because they're getting restless and impatient. This was tried at one ritual that I attended involving about 300 participants. It took almost an hour for the single chalice to make its way around the Circle.

Experienced people will substitute alternatives to overcome these difficulties. Using this example, the ritual leader(s) might first bless the cakes and wine, then allow everyone to come up after the ritual to collect a portion for themselves at their convenience. Alternatively they may circulate several chalices and platters to make the distribution occur more quickly.

Here's another example of poor planning. A very common scenario that I've seen over the years is the coven that plans to do an outdoor ritual and doesn't tell the local police. Often the local police department doesn't even know that there is a Wiccan coven in the neighborhood. Eventually some pedestrian who has watched too many "investigative reports on Satanism" or Hollywood horror movies sees the unsuspecting Wiccans dancing in a circle around a fire. This frightened citizen assumes that the neighborhood is being taken over by the legions of Satan. The citizen sprints to the nearest pay phone and calls 911. The police arrive, primed to believe that a Satanic ritual is in progress. They walk cautiously up to the ritual site, probably with their hands on their sidearms. They've probably seen the same television tripe as the pedestrian complainant. The Wiccans see the officers approaching. The High Priestess draws her athame to cut a doorway in the Circle so that she can go out and meet them. Suddenly we have a number of quivering cops with fingers on hair triggers aiming at a bewildered woman with a knife in her hand.

It's a miracle no one has been killed yet. Yet situations similar to this have happened all over North America. They happened because the organizers didn't foresee this problem. They didn't make any effort to introduce themselves to the local police. They didn't notify them of their gathering or get the permits necessary to hold one. It's a lot easier for a Witch to explain themselves to some cop or bureaucrat in the safety of an office somewhere beforehand, than to have to play catch-up at gunpoint later.

Here is another key point. No dogma is worth getting shot for. The world won't come to an end if you don't cut your way out of that Circle in those circumstances. A Wiccan Warrior would have assessed the situation first. Then he would have walked up to the edge of the Circle, or further if asked to, and explained the situation to the police without foolishly brandishing what looks like a weapon. I could provide plenty of other examples, but I'm sure you see my point. If possible, the Warrior leaves nothing to chance. This is part of the process of taking charge of your life.

What kind of contingencies must the designer of a ritual consider when writing a ritual? Blacksun identified a number of elements that must be present in any successful ritual:[8]

1. Decide on a precisely defined goal.
2. Establish the area.
3. Consecrate the area.
4. Crystallize the vision.
5. Raise the energy.
6. Focus, direct, and release the energy.
7. Ground stray energy.
8. Break the connections.

In the next chapter is an example of an initiation ritual I have used, and in the appendix at the end of the book is a Warrior Initiation Ritual. You may use them if you like, but I encourage the reader to try designing rituals of their own. However, one special type of ritual deserves a chapter to itself. In the next chapter we'll discuss initiations.

Endnotes

1. Shakespeare, William. *King Henry V*, Act IV, i, 256.

2. Bonewits, Isaac. (1979) *Real Magic*. Creative Arts Book Co., Berkeley, CA, p. 221.

3. Millman, Dan. (1984) *The Way of the Peaceful Warrior: A Book That Changes Lives*. H. J. Kramer, Inc., Tiburton, CA, p. 113.

4. Blacksun. (1988) *Three Times Around The Circle*. Self-published, pp. 5–11.

5. Hope, Murry. (1988) *The Psychology of Ritual*. Element Books, Dorset, p. 7.

6. McFarland, Phoenix. *The Complete Book of Magical Names*. Llewellyn, St. Paul, MN, p. 35.

7. McFarland, Phoenix. *The Power of Names*. p. 23.

8. Blacksun, pp. 57–73.

10

THE INITIATED WARRIOR

The Initiatory Experience

There is stick-to-it-iveness and there is getting entangled; stick-to-it-iveness is strength and entanglement is weakness. You must know the difference.[1]

—Miyamoto Musashi

T HERE IS A connection between the life stages in the development of a person following the Wiccan path and the three degrees of initiation. These stages and their corresponding degrees could be illustrated by looking at a typical young aspiring person who has studied and decided to dedicate themselves to the Wiccan way of life. This is the true first degree: commitment. Later, having learned and matured, the Wiccan starts to assist others starting on this path, beginning to teach and to assume the role of a sister/brother/leader. This is the second degree. Finally the Wiccan enters the crone/elder phase, becoming an advisor for less senior Wiccans. This is the third degree. Many women view these "life-stages" as Maiden, Mother and Cronehood. However you label these life phases, you don't necessarily need an initiation to enter them. The founder of Jeet Kune Do, Bruce Lee, put it this way: "Maturity does not mean to become a captive of conceptualization. It is the realization of what lies in our innermost selves."[2]

When I first got involved in Wicca, I discovered that most denominations of Wicca had these three established degrees of initiation. Theoretically a person studying one of these traditions will move upward until they arrive at the third and final degree. This then gives them the authority to go out and start a coven of their own. Each degree entitles the initiate to wear a particular color cord to designate their rank, the color varying between different traditions and covens. This would be a familiar system to a student of the martial arts. Most martial arts schools have established grading systems through which a student must progress to become a master, marked by different colored belts.

Most martial arts schools using the degree system will tell you that a person must go through rigorous training and achieve certain training objectives before being passed on to the next level in their tradition. This is the primary justification for the degree system; it allows you to grade people according to their level of mastery of the knowledge required. But this practice is only about seventy years old. Originally all you got was a white belt. With wear, tear, and age it slowly turned brown, then black. By that time you were probably a master. Eventually the belt became frayed, loosening the threads and turning it white again. It was impatient people in the Western world who wanted signposts to mark their progress.

Unfortunately this grading process is a rather arbitrary process in many Wiccan groups. Not all of them actually take the time to list the requirements for each degree and draw up a training syllabus that reflects these requirements. There has been no widespread collaboration between groups to standardize the requirements. And some leaders use their own petty and sometimes vindictive reasons for giving or withholding elevation, which is far from fair.

Consequently the standards vary enormously between groups. Often training consists of simply parroting information that anyone could have obtained on their own from easily available books. Sometimes the process used to determine acceptability for initiation is quite arbitrary, being mainly a matter of who is in favor, and who is not.

As I mentioned earlier, some covens, trying to form themselves into a religious organization recognized by the state or federal government, have found themselves scrambling to meet requirements set by law. These are usually requirements set by a Christian society, not a Pagan one. To get ministers' credentials, Wiccans may find themselves modeling their degree standards after a system imposed by (Christian) society. The bottom line is that although some people can produce a certificate (suitable for framing) announcing their third-degree initiation, often there is little or no chance of ever proving: (a), they went through any kind of meaningful training to earn it; and (b), that they did not print it up themselves. In my years of antidefamation work I've received numerous letters and phone calls from people complaining that "so and so" of their acquaintance didn't really have the initiations they claimed to have. Often it came down to credibility; one person's word against another.

More and more I run into Witches who are almost fanatical in their insistence upon seekers acquiring a degree from a mainstream denomination of Wicca. I've met more than a few Wiccan "teachers" who were trying to validate themselves by publicizing the lineage of their initiators. As pointed out above, some of them stretch the truth a little in their urgent quest to establish this lineage. Thus, we are seeing the formation of a series of apostolic successions. People trying to become respectable by apostolic association rather than by earning respect. Sound familiar? Isn't this just another form of "older is better" stuff?

The aspiring student is sometimes made to feel that unless she obtains a degree from such a teacher, her position within the Wiccan community will be that of an impertinent, insolent upstart. They are often made to feel that they have no "official status," that they are somehow illegitimate. The real losers in this situation are the solitary practitioners. They are often ostracized, looked down upon as illegitimate second cousins by those holding some manner of degree or other. Unfortunately, some then feel pressured into inventing some sort of initiation for themselves, performed by some obscure person or long-dead relative to try to justify themselves. They feel pressured into seeking to gain acceptance from the established groups. This is ironic, since some of the most powerful Witches I know are solitaries. Many have never had any "formal" training.

This system of initiates versus noninitiate tends toward radical cliquishness, and could become a real problem a few decades down the road. This is what fuels the kind of conflicts we see in Northern Ireland and the Middle East: Catholics vs. Protestants, fundamentalists vs. moderates. "My way is better than your way." The human desire to exclude is very strong. Robert Moore described it this way, "As a species we are still afflicted by the phenomena of projection and pseudo-speciation, which tempt us to experience others as the Enemy and ourselves as the righteous. When we project, we make others bear our own Shadows."[3]

You see, as I said at the beginning of this chapter, the point of the degree system and of initiation is that it is supposed to enable the student to master a particular art. Acquiring a degree or initiation is meaningless unless it really indicates a certain mastery has been attained. Through commitment, discipline, study, and hard work, one can achieve mastery in Wicca without ever having attended a Wiccan Circle or having ever received an "approved" initiation from any apostolic succession of clergy. If you haven't mastered your practice of Wicca, it doesn't matter how long an apostolic succession you have behind you.

I believe that Wicca is supposed to be a religion that allows us to find out what works for us, because we are all different. Vive la différence! You do not become a Witch by deciding to join some exclusive Wiccan clique. You become a Witch by making a decision to live as one. You join a coven because it has attributes that complement your own and valuable lessons to offer you. It makes no difference whether it is part of an established tradition or not. The longest lasting coven of my acquaintance was formed by a group of seekers who got together and read all they could on Wicca. They experimented. They all took turns as High Priest or Priestess, and regularly practiced their craft. They don't waste time playing the "Witchier-than-Thou" game. As it turns out, they ended up with a far better coven with better results than many of their multidegreed counterparts, and they certainly had more fun.

Wicca ought to be a truly democratic religion in which we are all treated as equals. Respect is not bestowed upon a person by giving them a third-degree certificate. It is something that is earned. And the Wiccan Warrior keeps on earning it by their behavior and personal standards of conduct.

So should we then dump the degree system? Not necessarily. Many groups use it effectively. But it requires leaders and teachers who are confident, knowledgeable, and not looking for self-aggrandizement. And even if you've got these kind of people, degrees are certainly not obligatory. Musashi, who trained himself, became a master swordsman who was never defeated. I'm reminded of the scene in the movie *The Karate Kid* where the young man asks his mentor what belt he has. The teacher looks at the belt on his pants and says, "J. C. Penney, $1.49." In the final analysis, do all of those colored belts and certificates amount to much? Not very.

So why do an initiation at all? And what is an initiation anyway? Let's look at the following definition:

> *Initiate,* v.t.; initiated, pt., pp.; initiating, ppr.[from L. *initiatus,* pp. of *initiare,* to enter upon, initiate, from *initium,* a beginning.] 1. to bring into practice or use; to introduce by first doing or using. 2. to teach the fundamentals of some subject to; to help (someone) to begin doing something. 3. to admit as a member into a fraternity, club, etc., especially through use of secret ceremony or rites. Syn.—begin, commence, start, install, induct, inaugurate.[4]

Many Wiccan groups use initiation as it is defined in the third definition: as admittance into "a fraternity, club, etc., especially through use of secret ceremony or rites." Here is what Stewart Farrar states in Volume II of *A Witches' Bible* regarding first-degree initiation: "In a formal sense, first-degree initiation makes you a rank and file witch."[5] He goes on to say that first-degree initiation can also be "a two-way gesture of recognition and acknowledgment and, of course, a ritual of welcome to a valued addition to the coven. . . . It can give them a sense of belonging, a feeling that an important milestone has been passed; and just by giving a sincere postulant, however apparently ungifted, the right to call himself or herself a witch, you are encouraging him or her to work hard and to live up to the name."[6]

Is Farrar suggesting that we are simply inducting a person into the "rank and file" of a structured organization, a bureaucracy, where members are organized by ranks (degrees)? Gardner said that there was no such structure. Is this like joining the Marines? The way that Farrar words this statement hints at an almost military hierarchy. Is the new initiate simply "a valued addition to the coven?" This implies that recruiting new members is an important task. Yet Wiccans aren't supposed to proselytize. The last part sounds absolutely condescending in its tone. We feel sorry for you, so we'll give you the name and hope that you work hard to live up to it.

Initiatus, (pp. of *initiare*), to enter upon, initiate, from initium, a beginning. Initiation *isn't* just a membership ceremony. You can experience an initiatory experience without the assistance of *any* group. The solitary vision quest of the First Nations Peoples of North America is just one example. You can experience a group initiatory experience such as the Greek Mysteries of Eleusis and not become a member of anything. Initiation is a rebirth. A beginning. Entering into a new phase, striking out on a new adventure, setting out on a new path. Like the Fool in the Tarot's Major Arcana. It is an individual experience, although several individuals can experience it in the same time and place. It brings about a change of consciousness. By this definition, the initiation ceremony must be created to facilitate this change in consciousness, this new beginning.

To be fair, Farrar indicates that he recognizes this on the next page, stating: "Every initiation, in any genuine religion or fraternity, is a symbolic death and rebirth, consciously undergone."[7] Many structured religions have institutionalized initiations, turning it into an unalterable ceremony. Some of these, like the Mysteries of Eleusis, were very successful, continuing in an unbroken tradition for over 1,000 years and recently being revived by the groups like the Aquarian Tabernacle Church in Seattle. But no matter how institutionalized they become, each initiation always differs in at least subtle ways from every other, taking on characteristics of the initiators and the setting in which the initiation is performed. The danger of using such a system is that the initiators may come to regard their task as simply the performance of a membership ceremony. Thus, the initiation, no matter how elaborate, may fail utterly to bring about the change of consciousness, the new beginning that it represents.

Some religious systems make the initiatory experience a solitary one, setting up the conditions to allow the initiate to achieve his or her objective alone and unaided. That such initiations work is ample proof that much of the dogma surrounding institutionalized initiation ceremonies is largely unnecessary.

One of the most effective techniques is to write an initiation specifically for the individual it is intended for. I'll give you an example of an initiation that we wrote for one of our friends. Then I'll compare it with a "standard" Wiccan-style initiation so that you'll see how we put it together with the specific purpose of cause a change in the initiate's consciousness.

First we had to take a good look at the initiate and decide what sorts of things "spoke" to him; we wanted to know what caught his imagination. He was a young, "hippie" sort of fellow, who was born in Germany. He was deeply moved by an American Aboriginal past life. For him, an initiation involving elements of American Indian tribal spirituality would be meaningful. He had never experienced a "skyclad" ritual before. We anticipated that including these elements would create an intensity of experience for his initiation.

Another thing that captured our attention involved an experience that my wife and best friend Phoenix had a few years back, which she had described to this initiate. She had been floated along a pool in darkness, passed on from one person to the next as these individuals lovingly caressed her and spoke gently to her, and aromatic things like

rose petals were held under her nose. It involved all the senses by block-
ing off some to enhance others. The fact that it was an initiation to a
nudist camp in California held in a pool did not diminish the success of
this initiation. This initiate had been very moved by the description of
this ritual and had expressed a desire to have something like this happen to him some day. We made a note of this. Sometimes you have to
be careful about touching others because they are uncomfortable about
it, but this was obviously not a concern here.

We planned the initiation to take place on the first evening of a major
festival in Colorado called Dragonfest. There were two reasons for this.
Firstly it would require the initiate to travel from British Columbia to
Colorado on his own, giving him the sense of going on a vision quest, the
first of two tasks he had to accomplish. This was a significant step for
him, because apart from being brought to Canada from Germany as an
infant, he had never traveled. Secondly it would allow us to use the help
of some Wiccans in the Denver community who had talents vital to this
initiation. These Wiccans came from several different traditions, and a
few of them were solitary Wiccans we respected. None of the solitaries
that we asked had ever been initiated into any tradition. Most of them
had never been allowed to witness one of any sort before, but there was
no question about any of them being dedicated to the Craft; they lived it.

The initiate met us at the festival site the day before, as we were part
of the festival set-up crew. The initiate was introduced to the fourteen
people who were to be participants in his initiation. In fact, he worked
alongside them setting up much of the festival site. By getting to know
them in this way he felt part of their community and learned that they
were to be trusted. There would be no surprises for him in this regard.
We left very specific instructions with these participants *not* to give him
a hard time or tease him about the initiation. I've seen some covens
take every opportunity to try to scare the wits out of an initiate before
the ceremony begins and I consider this childish and irresponsible. I
know what it's like; this hazing was done to me when I was a novice. In
the end it turned out that these precautions probably weren't necessary,
as we had chosen the people to assist us well and they were mature

enough not to engage in such activity. The second task that we had given the initiate was the task of choosing a new name for himself. He was not to reveal it to anyone until his initiation.

The site for this Circle was a small clearing in a grove of aspens and pines by a brook in the Colorado Rockies. The ritual was to take place after dark, and we set out chemical light sticks, or "glow sticks," to mark the trail to the site. We didn't want any of the participants to get lost in the wilderness. The initiate would be taken to a place about 100 meters away from the site. It was on the other side of a slight rise, so that he would not be able to see or hear what was going on until we were ready.

At the entrance to the Circle we set up a tunnel. We used a child's toy, a spiral spring with a plastic cover making a flexible tunnel about seventy centimeters in diameter. We purchased two of these, each of them three meters long, and placed them end to end in a winding path. They were lined with soft blankets, and a kerosene camp heater was used to warm it up inside.

After the festival opening ritual, the initiate was taken to the place where he would wait. We left him there to meditate on the initiation he was about to experience. Meanwhile, the participants met at the grove. After the Circle was cast, the men all filed down the path to where the initiate awaited. The women remained behind. About a dozen yards away from the initiate, the men stopped and I went on alone to where the initiate had risen to his feet. He stripped off his clothes, symbolic of the nakedness of the newborn. He was allowed to retain his boots, since we didn't want him to cut his feet. Suffering of this sort isn't necessary in this sort of initiation. At this point I asked what name he had chosen and heard for the first time the new name that he wanted to be known by. I then blindfolded him, using a sleeping mask. This put the initiate in a rather helpless state, at the hands of those initiating him, but as pointed out earlier, he knew them and had reason to trust them. As I slipped the blindfold onto him I said:

In the beginning there was darkness, formlessness, and chaos.

The men now gathered around him. I had supplied each of them with a face-painting crayon, and they proceeded to mark whatever designs came to them on his body. I had reserved a green crayon, and as his sponsor reserved the right to paint his face, drawing a leafy Green Man mask. As we painted his skin, we softly chanted his name, the volume gradually rising to a crescendo. It then suddenly subsided, and the men began to whisper whatever knowledge or advise they felt moved to give him. They told him about love, about strength, and about life.

While this was happening, one man broke away to tell the women what the initiate's chosen name was. The women silently positioned themselves at intervals along the path between the initiate and the Circle. Each woman carried a dime store toy, a plastic "microphone" with a diaphragm in it that made one's voice reverberate when you spoke or sang into it. They looked funny, but the initiate couldn't see them. He would only be able to hear the sound effect they created. One woman held a Tibetan singing bowl in readiness.

Seeing that the women were ready, the men withdrew as silently as they had arrived, drifting up the path to the Circle to get ready for the next part. As I backed away from the initiate, I told him:

> If you seek the Goddess, you must listen for her voice! You must follow her voice!

The initiate was left standing for a moment and then the woman with the singing bowl started to play it, filling the air with its ringing drone. The closest woman to him began to softly call.

> (Initiate's name)! I am the Goddess. I am Demeter! Come to me! Follow me!

The initiate slowly walked forward toward the woman, who continued to call until he was almost in front of her. She then stepped aside and the next woman up the path began to call:

(Initiate's name)! I am the goddess! I am Brigid! Come to me!
Follow me.

Each woman in turn repeated this process, each taking the persona of
a different Goddess of their choice. Hestia, Aphrodite, Persephone, Rhiannon, Athena, and Iris all made appearances. They said to him whatever they were moved to say in their roles as Goddesses. The initiate was
thus drawn up the path toward the Circle. It happened that the women
who were not actively calling him, who were really being moved by this
experience, began to spontaneously croon a melody softly, accompany-
ing the singing bowl. The effect made my hair stand on end. The initiate
was gradually led to the entrance of the tunnel described earlier.

One man, an experienced drummer, began to simulate the sound of
a heartbeat with his drum. Several men straddled the tunnel. Without
any words or warning the initiate was stopped by the women and made
to get on his hands and knees. He was then gently pushed into the tunnel. The singing and singing bowl abruptly stopped and the women,
lining up along the sides of the tunnel, began to give forth primal birth-
pang cries, deep breathing sounds, and moans. The men straddling the
tunnel pushed on either side of the tunnel simulating contractions
pushing him along.

The initiate told me later that when he first entered the tunnel he
was very rational, realized what kind of prop was being used and
understood what the women were trying to simulate. About halfway
through the tunnel his rationality deserted him. The tunnel was longer
than he expected, the "contractions" were unexpected, and suddenly it
wasn't a child's plastic tunnel anymore. He was fighting to escape the
birth tunnel, reliving his birth.

The women gathered near the end of the tunnel as he approached it.
They were chanting in quick succession: "I am Demeter! I am Persephone! I am Aphrodite! I am Brigid!" The chants became blurred
together, being replaced as the initiate emerged with chanting in unison: "I am! I am! I am! . . ." As he struggled to his feet, silence fell.

The woman who had played Aphrodite then stepped in front of him and, taking the initiate by the hand, led him forward and said: "Come and lie upon my body, feel me beneath you and hear my heartbeat." She led the initiate over beside a fire we had burning and helped him to lay facedown on the bare earth beside it where it was warmer. The initiate later told me that when she had done this he had expected some sort of sexual rite between him and the woman leading him, such as a Gardnerian Great Rite. Imagine his surprise when he found himself hugging the Goddess herself, the Earth!

Meanwhile, the other participants collected their drums (one of the reasons that we had asked them all to participate is that they were all drummers). They all gathered around the initiate. The man who had done the heartbeat drumming led us, beginning the drumming by pounding a large frame drum directly above the initiate's back. The others joined in, directing the waves of percussion down the length of his body. The drumming lasted only a few minutes, but its power vibrated through the initiate, washing him with sound. At the signal of the heartbeat drummer we suddenly ceased.

At this point one woman began to play a gentle, soothing melody on her harp. The drums were set aside. Gentle, soft voices spoke the initiate's name, and we all touched him gently with our hands, caressing his back, legs, buttocks, hair, arms, etc., a Pagan "laying on of hands" like the one he had dreamed about. After a few minutes the initiate was encouraged to sit up slowly and offered a warm drink. He was then slowly helped to his feet by the group and positioned facing the fire.

Each of the women then recited a line of the Charge of the Goddess from the Gardnerian rite:

> I who am the beauty of the green Earth and the white moon upon the mysteries of the waters, call upon your soul to arise and come unto me. For I am the soul of nature that gives life to the universe. From me all things proceed. And unto me they must return. Let my worship be in the heart that rejoices. For behold! All acts of love and pleasure are my rituals. Let there be beauty and strength,

power and compassion, honor and humility, mirth and reverence within you. And you who seek to know me, know that the seeking and yearning will avail you not, unless you know the mystery. For if that which you seek, you find not within yourself, you will never find it without. For behold!

I had held a mirror up in front of the initiate's face while this recital began. As the word "behold" was said, Phoenix removed the initiate's blindfold, so that he was suddenly confronted with his face in its Green Man paint. The entire group then continued in unison:

For behold! I have been with you from the beginning, and I am that which is attained at the end of desire.

The initiate was then presented to the quarters by Phoenix, who then lead him to the center and addressed him:

"You have studied with us for more than a year and a day. You have begun to help teach beginners. You came to us asking for initiation. Tonight, you have been reborn into the Craft, have lain upon the Earth and joined with deity, have seen the God in your own face and have spoken to the Goddess herself. You are now a Priest of the Craft. In other religions, the postulant kneels while the Priest, towers above him. But in our tradition we are equals. I choose to kneel before you in respect, to welcome you." Phoenix then gave the initiate the five-fold kiss:

Blessed be your feet that are set upon Her path.
Blessed be your knees, which hold you proud and strong.
Blessed be your phallus, which dances to Her rhythm.
Blessed be your heart, which dances to your own.
Blessed be your lips, through which the God may speak.
Blessed be (initiate's name), child of the Goddess and the God and Priest of the Craft.

Phoenix then anointed the initiate with oil in a pentagram pattern: touching forehead, then left hip, then right shoulder, then left shoulder, then right hip, then back to his forehead.

I then stepped up in front of the initiate and addressed him:

> In other traditions, the initiate is made to take oaths to the Priestess or Priest and his measure is taken and kept as a threat to bind him to his oath. In our tradition, we ask no oath from you. We take no measures, require no oath. For it is not to us that you are dedicating yourself this night, but to the Goddess and the God. If you do not keep your oath to them, it is to them and your karma that you must answer, not to us. The only person capable of keeping your promises is you. If you wish to make some oath to the Goddess now, before witnesses, please feel free to do so now.

At this point the initiate, in his own words, affirmed to the Goddess that he would be true to the Craft and his friends. I then continued:

> The oaths you spoke tonight are between you and the Goddess. In other traditions, blood is taken from the initiate to solemnize their oaths. You may choose to give a drop of blood to the Earth, to seal the oath you took tonight. You are not required to do so, this is entirely between you and the Goddess. Do you so choose?

The initiate said yes and I handed him a sterilized needle with which he punctured his thumb and let a drop of his blood fall to the Earth. I then continued:

> Remember always, that you alone must take the responsibility for your actions.

At this point he was welcomed by all and presented with initiation gifts that we had brought for him. One of the gifts was a new robe, which he put on. Phoenix and I prepared "cakes and wine" and the initiate took it around to all who had participated. I then dismissed the quarters while everyone softly sang the old Pop song: "Na na na na, na na na na, hey hey hey, goodbye!" Everyone helped clean up and carry things back to the festival campsite. The glow sticks we used to illuminate the path were collected on the way back and handed out to kids at the festival.

The first major difference between this initiate's initiation and the standard Wiccan initiation is that in the standard Gardnerian system, a female postulant is initiated by the High Priest and a male postulant is initiated by the High Priestess. The initiator is always at least a second-degree Witch. Phoenix and I gave this procedure, and Gardner's reasons for it, a lot of thought, and decided to modify it.

First of all, Gardner's rationale for having a person initiated by a member of the opposite sex was based primarily on sexual polarity. Gardner placed great emphasis on the members of covens being paired up in perfect heterosexual pairs. Now a female may be able to teach a male many things, sex not the least. But if a male wants to know about male mysteries, about what it is to be a priest, then he should go to male priests. This is the way that it has been done in many ancient tribal societies. Since a priest is what we were about to make this initiate into, then it would be priests who prepared him for initiation.

Secondly, another difficulty that we had with Gardner's sexual polarity thing is that some covens consist of members of just one sex or members who are bisexual or homosexual. Gardner's system ignores their needs completely. We can't really blame Gardner for this. People were a lot more uptight about that sort of thing in Gardner's day.

Finally, I believe that it is best if *everybody* in Circle participates in *every* ritual. Ours was an initiation in which everyone had a vital part. In a standard Wiccan ritual, most of the ritual activity is done by the Priestess and Priest while everyone else either stands around or engages in directed group activity. Notice that in this initiation everyone had a part, and everyone was given the freedom to say what they were moved to in their own words, from the heart. The women chose to represent whatever Goddess suited them, so long as each of them represented a different one. So instead of being initiated by a particular person, this initiate was born into the Craft by the efforts of the community. We *all* welcomed him in.

Unlike the common Wiccan Initiation, this initiate was not bound in any way. In the Gardnerian rite, the postulant is bound with three cords: one nine-foot cord is used to bind the postulant's wrists behind his back, one end being wound around his neck and left to dangle, this end later being used as a leash to lead the postulant around. Another shorter cord is bound around the right ankle, and a final short cord is bound around the left knee with the ritual pronouncement: "Neither bond nor free." This is a Masonic custom and while I understand the symbolism involved, I disagree with it. I feel that an initiate chooses to be initiated. They come to us of their own free will. While the initiate may not know what to expect in our initiation, the initiate is unfettered by any person's will. I do not lead people around on leashes; that sends the wrong message to the initiate.

A touch you won't find in most Wiccan initiations is body painting. This was one of the parts that we knew would speak to the Native American dreams of our initiate. He later told me that he immediately realized what we were up to and it did give him the feeling of being the young tribesman being readied by the tribal Warriors. A very important aspect of this part of the ritual was the men's affirmation of him by verbally encouraging and passing on knowledge to him, building his self-esteem and confidence. Our religion is one of personal transformation and self-respect, not a religion of guilt and self-doubt.

We did blindfold this initiate, as is commonly done in Wiccan initiations. This is symbolic of the baby who is unable to see what awaits before it is born. The initiate enters naked (skyclad) too, as the baby enters the world. We have absolutely no rules about the participants as far as clothing goes however. In this initiation, it being rather chilly in the early evening at 9,000 feet in the Colorado Rockies in August, all of the participants (except for the initiate) wore robes. Some people that we discussed this with were upset, since they figured that all serious Wiccan ritual should be done skyclad. But my wife pointed out to them that to a nudist and former nude model like herself, nudity wasn't that special. It was more significant to her to don special ritual robes, as this spoke to her subconscious more strongly, signaling that we were about to create a sacred space. Remember that you're trying to cause changes in consciousness, including yours. Gardner was a nudist and this was a very shocking and unusual thing back in his day, so it had more of an impact then. Since the sexual revolution of the 1960s and 1970s, it isn't such a big deal for many people anymore.

The idea of having a voice lead the initiate to the Circle isn't new. I've seen it done in many different variations by other groups. In our case we wanted several Goddess voices to call him. This gives him the courage to go forward and trusting in the Goddess to lead him. He also learns that she appears in many guises, all of which are interrelated. At the end of the tunnel they all merge into one.

The birth tunnel idea isn't new either. For example, when I was initiated in a Georgian coven, I was passed through the legs of the coveners, who were all standing in a row, to simulate the same thing. We simply felt that the tunnel was a better prop for this.

In many Wiccan initiations, the postulant is challenged by a Priest or Priestess holding a knife against his or her chest at the entrance to the Circle. I heartily dislike the idea of using fear and the threat of physical violence in this kind of initiation. The idea behind this in the Gardnerian rite is that it was once customary to do this in the Burning Times, to test the sincerity of the postulant. But as I pointed out earlier, we know that Gerald's Book of Shadows doesn't really date from this era, despite its being written in an archaic sounding style of English in an attempt to make it look as if it were. This challenge is just part of the theatrical touches put in by Gardner to give it that archaic appearance.

There is far too much violence in the world today. We were bringing this initiate into a community of love and trust. We didn't want threats in this type of initiation. In this context I felt that it was a perfect example of "power over." How can you enter a Circle in perfect love and trust if someone has just threatened you? By empowering our initiate beforehand we did "power-with" instead.

In a common Wiccan initiation, the postulant brings passwords, "perfect love and perfect trust," which he must give to the person with the knife to gain admittance. Given that we were not admitting him to some secret society, we didn't require the initiate to use secret passwords. Like the most Wiccans, we used the five-fold kiss, and like the Gardnerians, this is performed between members of the opposite sex in this case, since the initiate is heterosexual. You'll note that the wording was changed from the original. The first line isn't much different, but the second one is. Instead of talking about kneeling at sacred altars in obeisance, we affirm self respect by saying: "Blessed be your knees, which hold you proud and strong." The third line of the Gardnerian five-fold kiss is supposed to be sexual. But it is written in such a weak style to avoid offending the sensibilities of those of Gardner's era that we rewrote it to read: "Blessed be your phallus, which dances to Her rhythm." We felt that the next line should relate to the line before it and to refer to the emotions: "Blessed be your heart, which dances to your own." The last line of the Gardnerian verse states that the lips are merely to "utter the Sacred Names." As we believe that we all have a connection to the divine and that the deity is present in us, we felt that it would be more appropriate to say: "Blessed be your lips, through which the God may speak." If it had been a female postulant, the words could be changed to read, "through which the Goddess may speak."

Another thing that we threw out is the symbolic scourging that many Wiccan traditions do at this point of the initiation, using a soft silken cord or some such. Before they do this they ask the initiate if they are willing to "suffer to learn" or if they are willing to undergo an ordeal before taking an oath. While this may have fulfilled the needs or fantasies of Gardner and some early British Gardnerians, I do not see that it serves any useful purpose for most other Wiccans. Gently slapping a person with a soft cord isn't an ordeal. All the evidence points to this being a means of sexually arousing Gardner. Sexual arousal wasn't the purpose of this initiation and, in any case, I don't need this to get aroused. Worse, this part of the ritual is clearly symbolic of the domination of the initiator or Priest or Priestess over the initiate; the initiate trussed up and bound to the altar and the initiator scourging the initiate, "power over" stuff again.

Some Wiccans will argue that in subsequent initiations the initiate gets an opportunity to return the favor, scourging the initiator. I feel that this is a very bad role model and is nothing but Judeo-Christian "eye for an eye" stuff, *not* representative of Wiccan morality. There are plenty of ways to build ordeals into rituals, such as tests of strength or ingenuity that the initiate must overcome (for example, the Warrior's initiation you'll find in the appendix to this book). None of them require the initiate to be bound, and not one of them requires one person to punish another, symbolically or otherwise. Being humiliated and "whipped" by silken cords does not compare with a young man taking his first trip through two countries alone to get to his initiation. His trip turned out to have many trials and tests of will and character. It was a true ordeal.

Like the Gardnerians, we use a symbolic great rite, but instead of using a woman to represent the body of the Goddess, we chose to give him the body of the Goddess (the Earth). The pounding drums, of course, awaken the root chakra, awakening sexual energy. This was followed by our laying on of hands, to demonstrate our unconditional acceptance of him and our concern for him.

The Gardnerian Charge of the Goddess was read by all of the different Goddesses, reinforcing the idea of their being interconnected. We all said the last line together to demonstrate that we all recognized that she was a part of us, just as he could see that it was a part of him when he found the mirror in front of his face.

We did not take a measure of the initiate with a ribbon or cord as they do in many Wiccan initiations. True, they usually give it back, but only after a long speech about how in the old days this was a precaution, etc. They then make you take an oath never to reveal anything about the Craft to an outsider. They threaten that the measure that was taken could be used to perform magick against the initiate if he ever failed to keep his oath. In my opinion:

1. This is just another of the things that Gardner slipped in to make the Book of Shadows look as if it dated from the Inquisition.

2. Even if it did date from then, why take someone's measure if you are just going to give it back?

3. It is utterly ludicrous to make someone to swear never to reveal things that can be read by literally anyone with the money to buy one of dozens of readily available books in print about Wicca.

4. Here is "power over" stuff again.

Instead, our initiate made his own oath to the Goddess. If the initiate doesn't keep their word, it isn't me that they need to be concerned about. It's their karma. I feel that this emphasizes the point that the initiate has free will and is responsible for his own actions.

In many Wiccan traditions a great deal of time in their first-degree initiation is devoted to presenting the initiate with the tools of the Craft and explaining what they are all for. There are several reasons why we didn't do this:

1. We taught our initiate all about Wiccan ritual tools before he even asked to be initiated, so we didn't see any point in repeating it all in a ritual setting.

2. I feel that the words that the Gardnerian ritual calls for in the presentation of these tools are contradictory and often inappropriate. For example, the initiate is told that the magick sword is used to "dominate, subdue and punish all rebellious spirits and demons, and even persuade angels and good spirits. With this in thy hand, thou art the ruler of the Circle."[8] Later the athame is described as a "true Witch's weapon." The wand is described as being used to control "certain angels and genii." The scourge is described in contradictory terms as both a "sign of power and domination" and an instrument used "to cause purification and enlightenment."[9] Angels and demons are part of a Christian dualistic mythology. I didn't feel that they belonged in a Wiccan Circle. "Dominate, subdue, and punish . . . ruler of the Circle . . . sign of power and domination," this is all "power over" stuff.

3. All this part of the ritual really does is give the initiator further scope to perform in front of the other coven members, who stand by idle while this is all going on. This is the initiate's finest hour, not somebody else's.

Several people who were allowed to read the ritual before it was performed objected to it. These objections were very enlightening, because it showed me how many different things people expected from an initiation. Here are their objections, along with my comments on them:

1. *"Each initiation should be the same as the one you got. They should never change."* If we are all different, and if the objective is to cause a change in the initiate's consciousness, then it stands to reason that certain changes must be made to reflect these differences.

2. *"You shouldn't reveal all your secrets to anyone until you have to."* If this person is to be my sister/brother, then why must I keep secrets from him or her?

3. *"You shouldn't make it interesting and personal. It's all right if it's boring because what is really happening is a merging of the initiate's spirit and your spirit on the astral. If the students are upset because the ritual is boring, then you didn't teach them that the real work is being done on another plane."* The purpose of initiation, by any definition, has nothing to do with "merging of the initiate's spirit and your spirit on the astral." It's a new beginning, not a marriage ceremony. Any effective educator will tell you that if the lesson is boring, it's ineffective.

4. *"An initiation is supposed to be like a handfasting between the Priestess and the initiate."* This comment brings to mind the Christian concept of the nun marrying herself to God or Christ. If the initiate is in love with the initiator, then handfasting might be an option for them. Otherwise, first-degree initiation is not a marriage to anyone.

5. *"By sharing the lines in the ritual among all the participants you are giving away your power over the coven and the initiate and you don't want to give away your power."* It wasn't my power in the first place, friend! It's the gift of the Goddess and God. I don't want power over the members of my coven. They're my sisters and brothers. The power belongs to all of us. So let's *all* use it!

6. *"It isn't spiritual. It's a pageant."* Pageants can be spiritual if you do them right. Ever attend a Catholic High Mass? The aforementioned Eleusian Mysteries were a pageant and they worked very well for thousands of years.

7. *"You changed all the important stuff. It's not traditional."* I asked this person why the stuff I had changed was important. They didn't know and voiced objection #1 (above).

8. *"I don't approve of your giving up all your power, so I won't participate, but I'd like to come to the ritual as an observer."* It's kind of funny when you think about it. They were telling us that we were wrong, but were just dying to watch it in case we turned out to be right. We refused, telling this individual that if they weren't willing to participate, they should not bother coming.

Several doubters attended the ritual and came away with a different perspective. Many of them seemed to have fun. Many of them later admitted this ritual was very moving. It's going to affect different people in different ways because we're all different. Here the person we most wanted to move is the person we wrote the ritual for. If others were moved too, that's a bonus. The larger the group, the more likely that there is going to be a few people that your ritual doesn't reach. You can't please everybody. Again, you should do whatever works for you. If stock rituals from standard texts is what work for you, go for it. If not, it's time to get creative and think of something else.

Endnotes

1. Musashi, Miyamoto. (1988) *The Book of Five Rings.* Bantam Books, New York, NY, Introduction, p. 46.
2. Lee, Bruce. (1975) *Tao of Jeet Kune Do.* Ohara Publications, Inc., Santa Clarita, CA, p. 15.
3. Moore, Robert and Douglas Gillette. (1992) *The Warrior Within: Accessing the Knight in the Male Psyche.* HarperCollins, San Francisco, CA, p. 96.
4. *Webster's New Twentieth Century Dictionary of the English Language,* Unabridged, Second Edition, ©1970, p. 943.
5. Farrar, Stewart. *A Witches' Bible,* Volume 1. p. 9.
6. Ibid.
7. Ibid., p. 10.
8. Farrar, Stewart. *A Witches' Bible,* Vol. II, p. 19.
9. Ibid., p. 20.

11

CONCLUSION

Moderation? It's mediocrity, fear, and confusion in disguise. It's the devil's reasonable deception. It's the wobbling compromise that makes no one happy. Moderation is for the bland, the apologetic, for the fence sitters of the world afraid to take a stand. It's for those afraid to laugh or cry, for those afraid to live or die. Moderation . . . is lukewarm tea, the devil's own brew![1]

—Dan Millman's teacher, Socrates

I F YOU CHOOSE this Warrior's path, be diligent. Prepare yourself. Don't be haphazard about anything; being a Wiccan Warrior is a way of life, not a part-time occupation. Master Musashi put it this way, "You must walk down the path of a thousand miles step by step, keeping at heart the spirit which one gains from repeated practice with whomever one can get to practice with, and knowledge attained from whatever experiences you can come by, without impatience."[2]

There is an old magickal adage, "To Dare, To Will, To Know, To Keep Silent." To these I would add a fifth, "To Imagine." These are the cornerstones of the magick of the Wiccan Warrior. Let us examine how each of these aspects of magick interact together to form a functioning whole. One way to do this is to imagine that each of these five principles forms a side of a pyramid.

The Base: *To Know*

This is the base of the pyramid. The only way to control something is to understand it. The more you know about it, the more control you have over it. Knowledge is power. There is an old Japanese saying, "From one thing know ten thousand things." Sun Bear put it this way: "Once you have your foundation, knowledge, understanding, centeredness and beliefs, you can look at the world and see what is real and what is an illusion."[3]

What follows logically from this is that to have control of yourself you must "know yourself." To know yourself is to develop a personal inventory of all the skills that you possess, as well as those you will require. It is a matter of making an honest appraisal of yourself, listing your strong and weak points objectively and truthfully. You see this principle in other fields that concern the raising and directing of energy, such as Tai Chi, Shiatsu, or Acupuncture. Sun Tzu once wrote, "So it is said that when you know yourself and others, victory is not in danger; when you know sky and earth, victory is inexhaustible."[4]

I have labeled this principle "to know" rather than "knowledge" for a reason. Knowing is awareness. It is a dynamic process. Bruce Lee once said that "Knowledge is fixed in time, whereas, knowing is continual. Knowledge comes from a source, from an accumulation, from a conclusion, while knowing is movement."[5] It is this characteristic that links it with one of the other five principles: To Keep Silent.

First Side: *To Dare*

To dare is to have faith in yourself and your abilities, to let go of your inhibitions and doubts. Magick simply does not work for you if you don't believe that it will. As you hone your skills with practice, your experience and confidence will grow, allowing you to push yourself further than before. Remember the battle cry of the Templars: Be glorious!

My wife Phoenix once told me that she had great success in manifesting her desires when she was a novice practicing candle magick. That is, until she met someone who told her that they were very happy that almost half their spells worked. It never occurred to Phoenix that it might *not* work. After that, she had a much harder time making her magick spells work. "As soon as my doubt was kindled, I couldn't stop the blaze," she explained.

In many books on the art of being a Warrior, the awareness of death plays an important role. All of us suffer from a fatal disease: birth. We are all going to die. You haven't time to waste, to doubt, to procrastinate. The Warrior makes every moment count. He faces each challenge as if it is a life or death struggle. Nothing is unimportant. This is the spirit of daring that I'm talking about here. Don Juan Matus told his student Carlos:

> Use [the knowledge of your death]. Focus your attention on the link between you and your death, without remorse, or sadness of worrying. Focus your attention on the fact you don't have time and let your acts flow accordingly. Let each of your acts be your last battle on earth. Only under those conditions will your acts have their rightful power. Otherwise they will be, for as long as you live, the acts of a timid man. . . . It isn't [so terrible to be a timid man] if you are going to be immortal, but if you are going to die there is no time for timidity. . . . Being timid prevents us from examining and exploiting our lot as men. . . . Most people move from act to act without any struggle or thought. A hunter, on the contrary, assesses every act; and since he has an intimate knowledge of his death, he proceeds judiciously, as if every act were his last battle. Only a fool would fail to notice the advantage a hunter has over his fellow men. A hunter gives his last battle its due respect. It's only natural that his last act on earth should be the best of himself.[6]

Second Side: *To Will*

To will is to have an unwavering purpose and self-discipline. It is the channeling of your awareness to focus precisely on that which you want with burning intensity. If you don't know where you're going, then you'll probably arrive some place else. You must learn to clearly define your objective and to persistently work toward it. The Warrior is goal-oriented. Award-winning actress Cybill Shepherd recently stated that "As a woman out there today, you have to be a warrior. When I started in this business thirty years ago, nobody believed I could do what I do today. I did it by sheer not giving up."[7]

Self-discipline is the hallmark of the Warrior.[8] This is not merely a physical discipline such as one finds in the martial arts or in athletic competition. It also involves the training of the mind. Concentration is essential to magick. If you simply broadcast the energy that you raise in no particular direction, or with a very vague or general focus, it will not have much effect. But if all of your energy is focused on a very narrow purpose, or on a very clearly defined goal, it will invariably succeed. This is the same principle that makes a punch so effective in Karate; energy (Chi) is concentrated and focused with intent.

Third Side: *To Imagine*

To imagine is to be able to clearly visualize your objective, to develop and use a creative imagination. There is an old adage in magick, "Be careful what you ask for! You'll probably get it!" If you haven't carefully considered exactly what you want and/or have not been able to accurately visualize your goal, then what you ask for will probably not meet your expectations or requirements. So an accurate and creative imagination is essential to magick.

Dr. Jonn Mumford, a Western doctor trained in Eastern medicine and Yoga, teaches that to visualize something fully you have to build a "CASE":

1. The C stands for *Color.* Visualize an object in the most vivid colors that you can imagine.

2. The A stands for *Action.* Moving objects are always easier to focus on, just ask anybody who creates TV commercials. If you are visualizing an automobile, put it in motion, make the wheels spin.

3. The S stands for *Size.* In Western culture we imagine things as being rather small because we have been taught that one's consciousness

resides in the brain. It's as if we have to make the object small to fit inside our head. Instead, make the object that you are visualizing *huge.*

4. The *E* stands for *Emotion.* Recent studies into ESP and related phenomena have proven the old belief that such abilities (and magick) work best when the person(s) doing it are very emotionally involved in the process.[9]

Be careful how you do this. For example, when doing healing magick, one should always work with positive images rather than negative ones, to keep the focus clear. For example, if I said to you, "Do not think of a cat," your subconscious would conjure up an image of a cat so that you could see what it is I *don't* want you to see. Therefore thoughts like "be healthy" and "long life" would work better than "no more illness."

Fourth Side: *To Keep Silent*

The first of the five principles that we discussed was "to know." Knowledge comes from listening. "Silence is the warrior's art and meditation is his sword."[10] To keep silent is to become still within and without. To clear your mind of distractions. To become aware of subtle currents, instincts, and emotions. To become pure awareness. This allows the Wiccan Warrior to be ready to seize the opportunities that come, and to follow the path intuition leads him down. "Understanding is one-dimensional. . . . Realization, on the other hand, is three-dimensional."[11]

There is an old saying in Karate, "Mind like water, mind like the moon." The mind must be like a still pond, conscious of the slightest ripple, able to accurately reflect reality. Bruce Lee encouraged the warrior to "Observe what is with undivided awareness."[12] Satori is the Warrior's state of being. A mind free of thought. Pure awareness.

The Warrior must learn to wait patiently. This was a very important principle to the ancient Samurai. The weaker swordsman, unable to stand the strain of waiting, often tried to deal the first blow. In an instant he revealed his strategy to his opponent. It was only then that his more patient and skilled opponent would strike, using a blow that was a combination of parry and attack, calculated to neutralize the strategy revealed by the less-patient opponent. To stand face to face with an enemy armed with four feet of razor-sharp steel in this fashion required endless patience and awesome concentration. This endurance and diligence will intensify your magick.

Imagine that this "Witch's pyramid" encloses the energy that you use in your magick. You can see that a flaw in any side will cause the energy to leak out and weaken the magick's effect. The Wiccan Warrior hones her pyramid to seal up these flaws. At the same time, she seals up the flaws in her own character.

Miyamoto Musashi summed up his Heiho ("Path to Enlightenment") in nine principles:

First: Do not harbor sinister designs.
Second: Diligently pursue the path of Niten Ichiryu (Two-Swords-As-One).
Third: Cultivate a wide range of interests in the arts.
Fourth: Be knowledgeable in a variety of occupations.
Fifth: Be discreet regarding one's commercial dealings.
Sixth: Nurture the ability to perceive the truth in all matters.
Seventh: Perceive that which cannot be seen with the eye.
Eighth: Do not be negligent, even in trifling matters.
Ninth: Do not engage in useless activity.[13]

Being a Warrior is daring to be more than you thought you could be. It is daring to excel. It is wanting to be something better. It is taking charge of the process of change in your life, rather than letting the process of change take control of you. It is learning to raise energy and using it effectively to bring your dreams to fruition. It is being responsible and honorable. It is having the "right stuff" and doing the right thing. Don't settle for the status quo. Be glorious!

Endnotes

1. Millman, Dan. (1984) *The Way of the Peaceful Warrior: A Book That Changes Lives.* H. J. Kramer, Inc., Tiburton, CA, p. 133.

2. Musashi, Miyamoto. (1988) *The Book of Five Rings.* Bantam Books, New York, NY, Introduction, p. 52.

3. From a presentation given by Sun Bear in California in 1985.

4. Tzu, Sun, trans., Thomas Cleary. (1991) *The Art of War.* Shambhala, Boston, MA, p. 87.

5. Lee, Bruce. (1975) *Tao of Jeet Kune Do.* Ohara Publications, Inc., Santa Clarita, CA, p. 16.

6. Castaneda, Carlos. *Journey to Ixtlan,* pp. 84–85.

7. Shepherd, Cybill and Paula Yoo. (29 June 1998) "Meno-Peace: A Star Discovers That The Change Of Life Need Not Be One For The Worse," *People* magazine, Volume 49, No. 25, p. 74.

8. Moore, Robert and Douglas Gillette. (1992) *The Warrior Within: Accessing the Knight in the Male Psyche.* HarperCollins, San Francisco, CA, p. 110.

9. Mumford, Dr. Jonn. From *Creative Visualization* audiotape. Date unknown.

10. Millman, p. 82.

11. Ibid., p. 26.

12. Lee, p. 20.

13. Musashi, p. 25.

Appendix: Warrior Initiation

THE FOLLOWING INITIATION is adapted with permission from my wife's book, *The Complete Book of Magical Names*. This ritual requires five main participants (plus several hecklers) to take the following parts:

Boudicca: A Warrior queen of the Celtic Iceni tribe whose name means "victory." She is famous for having nearly defeated the Roman armies in an uprising to fight against the injustices done to her by the Romans occupying Britain in her time.

Cuchulainn: Legendary Warrior of Irish myth.

Scathach: The demi-goddess who taught Cuchulainn his Warrior skills.

Fionn Mac Cumhail: Another legendary Warrior. Captain of the Irish Fianna. The possessor of all knowledge after catching and consuming the mythical "salmon of knowledge."

The Morrigan: Irish Goddess of war and sexuality.

The candidate will have selected a suitable Warrior name by which he or she wishes to be known. As part of the Warrior initiation, he or she will take this new name. The candidate should dress in clothing which does not limit movement or entangle his or her limbs. Track pants, a sweatshirt, and running shoes are more appropriate for this ritual than robes.

The persons having roles in the initiation ceremony will take their places along a path. Boudicca will stand at the entrance to the path. She will be armed with a spear or a sword. Cuchulainn stands next along the path, his sword sheathed. Scathach, holding a spear, is the next along this path. Fionn Mac Cumhail is next, with a cauldron containing some sort of fruit beverage set beside him. The last person encountered along this path is the Morrigan.

The candidate will retire to a secluded place before the initiation ceremony in order to ground, center, and reflect on the approaching initiation. The candidate will know that it is time to approach the path to receive initiation when he or she hears a prearranged signal, such as a blast on a horn or the sound of drums. The sound of the drums will indicate to the candidate where the entrance to the path is located. As the candidate approaches the path, he or she will be challenged by Boudicca, who brandishes her weapon.

>*Boudicca:* "Hold! This is the path of the Circle of the Fianna, an army of Irish Warriors who swore their allegiance to the Ard Ri, the High King. They walked this earthly path many centuries ago, but their spirit lives on. This is also the path of the lucht lighe, the Ard Ri's personal guard, whose honor and dependability are renowned. None but Warriors may tread this hallowed place. I, Boudicca, the aire echta, represent the Ard Ri's personal champion. I am a champion of the oppressed, guardian of the gate. The lucht lighe, the embodiment of the Warrior's spirit, have gathered together in this magical place. We are Warriors all. Who approaches this hallowed place?"

The candidate gives his or her mundane name (not the Warrior name—that comes later). Boudicca steps up to the candidate and places the point of her weapon on the candidate's chest, saying: "What is your purpose here?"

The candidate states his or her desire to walk the path and be initiated as a Warrior in his or her own words.

Boudicca: "All on this path have faced a challenge or trial to make them worthy of the title 'Warrior.' What trials have you endured to earn your place here?"

The candidate briefly describes what challenges or trials he or she has overcome to improve his or her self.

Boudicca: "This is good. But all who enter this path are dedicated to something beyond themselves. Mere heroes are loyal to themselves. They seek to impress themselves and others. But the Warrior is loyal to a greater cause, and places this cause before his or her own interests. This is the first lesson of the Warrior: the lesson of transpersonal commitment. Have you learned this lesson? If so, to whom or to what do you pledge your fealty?"

The candidate states what he or she is loyal to.

Boudicca withdraws the point of her weapon from the candidate's chest and says: "This is good. Leave your blade outside this path, for on this path only Warriors may carry a blade."

The candidate turns over his or her athame to Boudicca.

Boudicca: "If you are truly determined to walk our path, [name of candidate], then start upon this path and learn the further mysteries of the Warrior's path in the company of the circle of the Fianna."

The candidate lead down the path by Boudicca and presented to Cuchulainn, who has his sword "Cruaiden Cadatchenn" ("little hard one"), in its sheath.

Cuchulainn: "Hold! I am Cuchulainn, the Hound of Ulster."

Cuchulainn draws his sword and paces around the candidate as he continues.

Cuchulainn: "I am the personification of action. I am the embodiment of energy. I am motivation made manifest. I am persistence and restlessness in pursuit of goals. I leap into battle with my full energy, and seize the day."

Cuchulainn stops in front of the candidate and asks: "Is it your intention to follow the Warrior's path?"

The candidate answers appropriately.

Cuchulainn: "Then I give you your first challenge: Before us on the path is a net staked tight to the earth. Using diligence, energy, persistence, and relentlessness, find a way to crawl under the net to achieve that which is waiting for you at the other end. A false, limited, and superficial person would wait until no one was looking and walk around to claim the prize falsely. A Warrior, however, would face the trial and crawl beneath the net to earn the prize. What say you, are you a Warrior or a cheat?"

The candidate answers appropriately.

Cuchulainn: "Then proceed with my blessing."

The candidate must crawl beneath a staked-out cargo net. Once the candidate reaches the far end, they will be encouraged by Boudicca to open the package, which will contain a suitable token of the candidate's achievement. Boudicca then takes the candidate further down the path to meet Scathach, who is armed with a spear.

Scathach: "Hold! I am Scathach, the tutor of Cuchulainn. I am the disciplinarian. I am the personification of control over mind and attitudes. Is it your intention to continue on the Warrior's path?"

The candidate answers appropriately.

Scathach: "Then I give you your second challenge: You are to remain still. You will not move, or speak, or look in any direction except straight ahead. You will not in any way abandon your concentration. You will remain immobile until I and only I come back for you. A lesser person might be distracted along the path, but a Warrior remains focused. Are you ready to begin your challenge?"

The candidate answers appropriately.

Scathach: "Very good. Then eyes forward, arms at your sides, your feet shoulder-width apart. Excellent. Don't move! Now gather your self-discipline and await my return."

After a minute of two, a group of hecklers comes along, one by one trying to distract the candidate from his or her stance. One might run up to the candidate shouting: "Hey! Scathach said follow me! Didn't you hear me? Let's go, candidate! *Move!* What are you waiting for? She said it was all right; now *move!*" Someone else might try to get the candidate to take a number of worthless dime-store trinkets from them, trying to convince the candidate to take them with statements such as: "Here! Take this! You'll need it ahead. Really!" Streamers or feathers can be waved in the candidate's face or used to touch them to elicit a response. Someone might sneak up behind the candidate and try to startle them with a yell. A person of the opposite sex might make sexual overtures to the candidate. The hecklers might try to get the candidate to say something or to draw them into an argument. A spouse or relative might come along and try to get the candidate to leave by saying: "What are you doing here? Get home this instant!"

If the candidate responds to any but Scathach, he or she will be encouraged to move along the path a short distance. Scathach will leap out, brandishing the spear and shrieking her ire. Scathach will herd the candidate back to where he or she was challenged and repeat the instructions. The candidate will then try again. If the candidate manages to stand without wavering for five minutes, Scathach returns.

Scathach: "Candidate! You have exerted great self-discipline and control over yourself and your emotions. You have acted as a Warrior might. You have earned this token."

A small gift is given. Boudicca next takes the candidate to Fionn Mac Cumhail, who stands by a cauldron.

Fionn: "I am Fionn Mac Cumhail, Captain of the Fianna. I am the personification of courage. To achieve courage, one must attain knowledge, judgment, and clarity of thinking. The Warrior knows what action is appropriate through clear thinking and discernment."

Fionn fills a cup from the cauldron and offers it to the candidate.

Fionn: "Drink then from the cauldron of courage. Learn about your strengths and weaknesses. The braggart does not know his or her limitations and romanticizes his or her invulnerability. The Warrior realistically assesses his or her capacities and limitations in every situation. Warriors know what they want and they know how to get it. The secret that enables a Warrior to reach clarity of thought is living with the awareness of his or her imminent death. Every act counts. This is the true meaning of courage. Is it your intention to continue on the Warrior's path?"

The candidate answers appropriately. Fionn retrieves the cup from the candidate.

Fionn: "Then I give you your third challenge."

Fionn points to a tree where a package has been placed on a high branch. A rope ladder or a simple rope (for the more youthful and athletic candidates) is provided to reach this package.

Fionn: "There is your goal. It is up to you to achieve it. A coward would shake the tree and cause the package to fall into his or her hands without effort. A manipulative person would get another person to go get the package, claiming illness, age, or fear as a reason that they could not do it. A Warrior would climb the rope (ladder) and attain the goal. Can you summon up the courage to scale these dangerous heights and achieve your goal?"

The candidate answers appropriately.

Fionn: "Then proceed with my blessings."

The candidate climbs the rope (ladder), claims the package, and climbs down with it. Boudicca encourages him or her to open the package and claim a token gift. Boudicca next takes the candidate to the Morrigan, who stands by a large stone.

> *Morrigan:* "I am the Morrigan, the Goddess of battle and destruction. I am a destroyer only of that which needs to be destroyed in order for something new and fresh, more alive and virtuous to appear. I obliterate corruption, tyranny, oppression, injustice, obsolete and despotic hierarchies, unfulfilling lifestyles and job situations, and bad relationships. I do this so that better civilizations, better ventures, and better relationships may take their place. A Warrior must have the ability to destroy his or her negative traits, to destroy obsolescence, tyranny, corruption, or oppression as needed. Destruction is a part of your life, or nothing better would ever spring up, new and fresh. As the darkness of night is necessary to understand the brilliance of the day, so destruction is to creation. Are you willing to destroy that which traps you? Are you willing to pull down your limitations and destroy your ignorance? Is it your intention to continue on the Warrior's path?"

The candidate answers appropriately.

> *Morrigan:* "Then I give you your final challenge. Get through this barrier symbolizing that which keeps you from the circle of the Fianna and your Warrior nature. Get past your limitations. A fool would deny the existence of any barrier. A conceited person would claim he or she didn't need to attain the circle of the Fianna and would ridicule those Warriors who attained it. But a Warrior would fight his or her way through all barriers to the attainment of self-respect. The choice is yours."

By any means the candidate must make his or her way through a barrier wall built of flimsy wood which will come down with repeated kicking. Words like "self-doubt," "ignorance," "foolishness," or any other words meaningful to the candidate can be painted on the wall.

Once the candidate gets past the barrier, Boudicca presents them with a final present. The candidate finds his or herself standing close to the circle of the Fianna. All of the characters of the ritual are standing within the circle. Boudicca returns the candidate's athame and then leads them into the circle from a doorway cut into the northeast. She leads the candidate to the altar. The candidate's gifts are placed on the altar.

Boudicca: "Have you chosen a Warrior's name for yourself?"

The candidate tells Boudicca the name he or she has chosen.

Boudicca: "Repeat after me: I, [candidate's Warrior name], will strive to nobility of cause, honesty of word, and faithfulness of heart. I will live by the motto of the Fianna: Truth in my heart, strength in my hands, and consistency in my tongue. I swear by all I hold sacred, that until the heavens with all its stars fall upon me, and the earth gives way beneath me, and the sea burst its bounds to drown the land, I will strive to live my life as a Warrior. If I prove false to my oath, then may my weapons turn against me and leave me at the mercy of the Goddess. Form this day forth, I will seek to live up to the mighty name of [candidate's Warrior name]."

Candidate repeats the oath. Boudicca embraces the candidate on completion of the oath.

Boudicca: "Welcome to this Warrior's circle. You have learned what it is to be a Warrior, but be ever mindful that there is more to you than this. Know that Warriors combine their skills with the skills of the king and queen, and practice sound leadership. Know that Warriors combine their skills with those of the Witch, to give them mastery and control over themselves and their powers. Finally, know that Warriors combine their skills with those of the lover. This gives the Warrior compassion and a sense of connectedness with all things. A Warrior knows that there is no greater power in all the world than that of love. To be a balanced, mature, and effective human, you must combine all four of these aspects."

A celebration follows.

BIBLIOGRAPHY

Items marked with an asterisk (*) are titles I recommend to Wiccan readers.

*Adler, Margot. *Drawing Down the Moon.* Beacon Press, Boston, MA. 1986.

Al-Anon Family Groups. *One Day At A Time In Al-Anon.* Al-Anon Family Group Headquarters, Inc., New York, NY. 1973.

*Amber K. *How to Organize a Coven or Magickal Study Group.* Nine Candles, Mt. Horeb, WI. 1983.

*———. *Treasury of Coven Activities.* Nine Candles, Mt. Horeb, WI. 1992.

*———. *True Magic: A Beginner's Guide.* Llewellyn Publications, St. Paul, MN. 1990.

Anderson, William. *Green Man: The Archetype of Our Oneness With The Earth.* Harper Collins, San Francisco, CA. 1990.

Barnes, L. K., ed. *The Necronomicon.* Avon Books, New York, NY. 1977.

Barnhart, Robert K., ed. *Barnhart Dictionary of Etymology.* H. W. Wilson Co., NY. 1988.

Barrett, Francis. *The Magus.* Carol Publishing Group, Secaucus, NJ. 1967.

Bell, Jessie Wicker. *The Witches Workbook: The Magick Grimoire of Lady Sheba.* Zebra Books, NY. 1975.

Blacking, John. *How Musical is Man?* University of Washington Press, Seattle, WA. 1973.

*Blacksun. *Three Times Around the Circle.* Self-published, Seattle, WA. 1988.

———. *The Spell of Making.* Eschaton Productions, Inc., Chicago, IL. 1995.

Bly, Robert. *A Little Book on the Human Shadow.* Harper & Row, San Francisco, CA. 1988.

———. *Iron John: A Book About Men.* Vintage Books, New York, NY. 1992.

Bolen, Jean Shinoda. *Goddesses in Every Woman.* Harper & Row, San Francisco, CA. 1984.

———. *Gods in Every Man.* Harper & Row, San Francisco, CA. 1989.

Bonewits, P. E. I. *Real Magic.* Creative Arts Book Co., Berkeley, CA. 1979.

Bradley, Marion Zimmer. *The Mists of Avalon.* Random House, New York, NY. 1982.

Bridges, Carol. *A Soul in Place: Reclaiming Home as Sacred Space,* Earth Nation Publishing, Nashville, IN. 1996.

Brownlee, Judith. *Pagan Parenting, Pagan Parents.* Denver, CO. 1987.

*Buckland, Raymond. *Buckland's Complete Book of Witchcraft.* Llewellyn Publications, St. Paul, MN. 1986.

———. *Practical Candle Burning.* Llewellyn Publications, St. Paul, MN. 1972.

*———. *Scottish Witchcraft: The History and Magic of the Picts.* Llewellyn Publications, St. Paul, MN. 1992.

*———. *The Tree: The Complete Book of Saxon Witchcraft.* Samuel Weiser, New York, NY. 1974.

*———. *Witchcraft From the Inside.* Llewellyn Publications, St. Paul, MN. 1971.

Budge, E. A. Wallis. *Amulets and Superstitions.* Dover Publications, New York, NY. 1978.

———. *The Egyptian Book of the Dead.* Dover Publications, New York, NY. 1967.

Burton, Sir Richard, trans. *The Kama Sutra of Vatsyayana.* Berkeley Publishing Group, New York, NY. 1984.

Cabell, James Branch. *Jurgen.* Dover Publications, Inc., New York, NY. 1919.

Campanelli, Pauline. *Ancient Ways: Reclaiming Pagan Traditions.* Llewellyn Publications, St. Paul, MN. 1991.

Campanelli, Pauline and Dan Campanelli. *Circles, Groves and Sanctuaries.* Llewellyn Publications, St. Paul, MN. 1992.

Campanelli, Pauline. *Wheel of the Year: Living a Magical Life.* Llewellyn Publications, St. Paul, MN. 1989.

Campbell, Joseph. *Myths to Live By.* Bantam Books, New York, NY. 1988.

———. *The Hero With A Thousand Faces.* Princeton University Press, Princeton, NJ. 1968.

———. *The Inner Reaches of Outer Space: Metaphor as Myth and as Religion.* Harper & Row, New York, NY. 1986.

———. *The Masks of God: Primitive Mythology.* Penguin Books, New York, NY. 1976.

———. *Transformations of Myth Through Time.* Harper & Row, New York, NY. 1990.

Campbell, Joseph and Bill Moyers. *The Power of Myth.* Doubleday, New York, NY. 1988.

Carmichael, Alexander. *Carmina Gadelica: Hymns and Incantations.* Lindisfarne Press, Hudson, NY. 1992.

Carnes, Mark C. *Secret Ritual and Manhood in Victorian America.* Yale University Press, London. 1989.

Castaneda, Carlos. *The Teachings of Don Juan: A Yaquis Way of Knowledge.* Simon & Schuster, Toronto. 1974.

———. *A Separate Reality.* Simon & Schuster, Toronto. 1976.

———. *Journey to Ixtlan.* Simon & Schuster, Toronto. 1976.

———. *Tales of Power.* Simon & Schuster, Toronto. 1976.

———. *The Second Ring of Power.* Simon & Schuster, Toronto. 1977.

———. *The Eagle's Gift.* Simon & Schuster, Toronto. 1981.

———. *The Fire From Within.* Simon & Schuster, Toronto. 1984.

———. *The Power of Silence.* Simon & Schuster, Toronto. 1987.

Cavendish, Richard, ed. *Man, Myth and Magic.* Marshall Cavendish, NY. 1995.

Chadwick, Nora. *Celtic Britain.* Newcastle Publishing Co., Inc. North Hollywood, CA. 1989.

———. *The Celts.* Penguin Books, New York, NY. 1971.

Cooper, J. C.. *An Illustrated Encyclopedia of Traditional Symbols.* Thames & Hudson Ltd., London. 1978.

Crowley, Aleister. *Magick in Theory and Practice.* Castle Books, New York, NY. date unknown.

*Crowther, Patricia. *Lid of the Cauldron: A Wicca Handbook.* Samuel Weiser, York Beach, Maine. 1984.

Cruden, Alexander. *Cruden's Complete Concordance.* Zondervan Publishing, Grand Rapids, MI. 1968.

*Cuhulain, Kerr. *The Law Enforcement Guide to Wicca: Third Edition.* Horned Owl Publishing, Victoria, B.C. 1997.

*Cunningham, Scott. *Wicca: A Guide for the Solitary Practitioner.* Llewellyn Publications. St. Paul, MN. 1989.

Dahl, Roald. *The Witches.* Puffin Books, Harmondsworth, Middlesex. 1983.

Davis, Pete. "Student Manual: Aquarian Tabernacle Church." Aquarian Tabernacle Church, Index, WA. 1990.

De Givry, Grillot. *Witchcraft, Magic and Alchemy.* Frederick Publications. 1954.

Delyth, Jen. *Keltic Mandala: Symbols Explained.* Dragon Space, Vancouver. 1990.

Denning, Melita and Osborne Phillips. *Astral Projection.* Llewellyn Publications, St. Paul, MN. 1987.

———. *Mysteria Magica.* Llewellyn Publications, St. Paul, MN. 1986.

Deren, Maya. *Divine Horsemen: The Voodoo Gods of Haiti.* Chelsea House, New York, NY. 1970.

Donner, Florinda. *The Witches Dream.* Pocket Books, New York, NY. 1986.

Dreyfuss, Henry. *Symbol Sourcebook: An Authoritative Guide to International Graphic Symbols.* Van Nostran Reinhold, New York, NY. 1984.

Dumezil, Georges. *Archaic Roman Religion, Vols 1 & 2.* University of Chicago Press, Chicago, IL. 1966.

Dwelly, Edward. *Dwelly's Illustrated Gaelic to English Dictionary.* Cairm Gaelic Publications, Edinburgh. 1988.

Eisler, Riane. *The Chalice and the Blade.* Harper & Row, San Francisco, CA. 1988.

Eliade, Mircea. *Rites and Symbols of Initiation.* Harper & Row, New York, NY. 1958.

————. *The Sacred & the Profane*. Harcourt Brace Jovanovich, Publishers, New York, NY. 1959.

Ellis, Peter Beresford. *Dictionary of Celtic Mythology*. Constable & Co., London. 1992.

Evans, Bergen. *Dictionary of Mythology*. Bantam Doubleday Dell Publishing Group, Inc., New York, NY. 1970.

Evslin, Bernard, Evslin, Dorothy, and Ned Hoopes. *The Greek Gods*. Scholastic Books Services, New York, NY. 1966.

Farmer, David Hugh. *The Oxford Dictionary of Saints*. Oxford University Press, Oxford. 1978.

*Farrar, Janet and Stewart Farrar. *Eight Sabbats for Witches*. Phoenix Publishing, Custer, WA. 1981.

*————. *The Witches' God*. Phoenix Publishing, Custer, WA. 1989.

*————. *The Witches' Goddess*. Phoenix Publishing, Custer, WA. 1987.

*————. *The Witches' Bible. Vols 1 and 2*. Phoenix Publishing, Custer, WA, 1987.

*Farrar, Stewart. *What Witches Do*. Coward, McCann & Geoghegan, Inc., New York, NY. 1971.

*Fitch, Ed. *Magical Rites from the Crystal Well*. Llewellyn Publications, St. Paul, MN. 1988.

Fodor, Nandor. *Encyclopedia of Psychic Science*. University Books, Fayetteville, AR. 1966.

Ford, Patrick K. *The Mabinogi and Other Medieval Welsh Tales*. University of California Press, Berkeley, CA. 1977.

Fortune, Dion. *Moon Magic*. Samuel Weiser, York Beach, ME. 1978.

————. *Psychic Self Defence*. The Aquarian Press, Wellingborough, Northamptonshire. 1981.

————. *The Demon Lover*. Wyndham Publications, Ltd., London. 1976.

————. *The Goat Foot God,* Samuel Weiser, York Beach, ME. 1980.

————. *The Sea Priestess*. Samuel Weiser, York Beach, ME. 1978.

————. *The Winged Bull*. Wyndham Publications, Ltd., London. 1976.

*Frazer, James G. *The Golden Bough: A Study in Magic and Religion*. MacMillan Press, New York, NY. 1971.

Frence, Peter. *John Dee: The World of an Elizabethan Magus.* Routledge & Keegan Paul, London. 1972.

Frost, Gavin and Yvonne Frost. *The Magic Power of Witchcraft.* Parker Publishing Co., West Nyack, NY. 1976.

———. *The Witch's Bible.* Nash Publishing, Los Angeles. 1972.

Gamache, Henri. *Mystery of the Long Lost Eighth, Ninth and Tenth Books of Moses.* Original Publications, Bronx, NY. 1983.

Gantz, Jeffrey. *Early Irish Myths and Sagas.* Penguin Books, New York, NY. 1981.

Gardner, Gerald. *High Magic's Aid.* Samuel Weiser, Inc., New York, NY. 1975.

*———. *The Meaning of Witchcraft.* The Aquarian Press, London. 1971.

*———. *Witchcraft Today.* The Citadel Press, Secaucus, NJ. 1974.

Gibson, Walter and Litzka Gibson. *The Complete Illustrated Book of the Psychic Sciences.* Doubleday, New York, NY. 1966.

Gimbutas, Marija. *The Goddesses and Gods of Old Europe.* University of California Press, Berkeley, CA. 1990.

González-Wippler, Migene. *A Kabbalah for the Modern World.* Llewellyn Publications, St. Paul, MN. 1987.

———. *Santería: African Magic in Latin America.* Original Products, New York, NY. 1981.

Goodman, Linda. *Sun Signs.* Bantam Books, New York, NY. 1970.

Grand Lodge of British Columbia, AF & AM. *History of Grand Lodge of British Columbia: 1871–1970.* Grand Lodge of British Columbia. 1971.

Grant, James. *Mysteries of All Nations.* Leith, Reid and Son, Edinburgh. 1971.

Graves, Robert. *The Greek Myths. Vols 1 and 2.* Penguin Books, New York, NY. 1955.

*———. *The White Goddess.* Farrar, Straus and Giroux. New York, NY. 1974.

Green, David and Richmond Lattimore, eds. *Greek Tragedies, Volume 2.* University of Chicago Press, Chicago, IL. 1960.

*Green, Miranda J. *Dictionary of Celtic Myth and Legend.* Thames and Hudson, London. 1992.

Guazzo, Francesco Maria and Montague Summers, eds. *Compendium Malefi-carum*. Dover Publications, New York, NY. 1988.

Guiley, Rosemary Ellen. *The Encyclopedia of Witches and Witchcraft*. Facts on File, New York, NY. 1989.

Hamilton, Edith. *Mythology: Timeless Tales of Gods and Heros*. New American Library, Inc. New York, NY. 1969.

Hart, Mickey. *Drumming at the Edge of Magic: A Journey into the Spirit of Per-cussion*. HarperCollins, San Francisco, CA. 1990.

———. *Planet Drum: A Celebration of Percussion and Rhythm*. Harper-Collins, New York, NY. 1991.

Hart, R. *Witchcraft*. Wayland Publishers Ltd., London. 1975.

Hawking, Stephen H. *A Brief History of Time: From the Big Bang to Black Holes*. Bantam Books, London. 1988.

Henrickson, Robert. *Encyclopedia of Word and Phrase Origins*. Facts on File. New York, NY. 1987.

Hinnells, John R. Ed. *The Penguin Dictionary of Religions*. Penguin Books, New York, NY. 1984.

Hoffman, Yoel. *The Sound of the One Hand*. Basic Books, Inc. New York, NY. 1975.

*Hole, Christina. *British Folk Customs*. Hutchinson & Co., Ltd. London. 1976.

Holzer, Hans. *The Witchcraft Report*. Ace Books, New York, NY. 1973.

Hope, Murry. *Practical Celtic Magic*. The Aquarian Press, Wellingborough, Northamptonshire. 1987.

———. *The Psychology of Ritual*. Element Books, Shaftesbury, Dorset. 1988.

Howard, Michael. *Candle Burning: Its Occult Significance*. The Aquarian Press, London. 1975.

Hulse, David Allen. *The Key of It All*. Llewellyn Publications, St. Paul, MN. 1993.

*Hutton, Ronald. *The Pagan Religions of the Ancient British Isles*. Basil Black-well Ltd., Oxford. 1991.

*Johnson, Charles. *The Sorcerer's Apprentice*. Penguin Books USA Ltd., New York, NY. 1994.

Jung, Carl G. *Analytical Psychology: Its Theory and Practice.* Routledge & Kegan Paul, London. 1986.

―――. ed. *Man and His Symbols.* Dell Publishing Co., Inc. New York, NY. 1964.

Keen, Sam and Anne Valley-Fox. *Your Mythic Journey.* Jeremy P Tarcher, Inc. Los Angeles. 1973.

*Kelly, Aidan. *Crafting the Art of Magic, Book I: A History of Modern Witchcraft. 1939-1964.* Llewellyn Publications, St. Paul, MN. 1991.

*―――. *Diana's Family: A Tuscan Lineage and Aradianic Faerie Tradition.* Pictish Voodoo Distributing Co., CA. 1993.

*―――. Hippie Commie Beatnik Witches: The California Craft 1967-1977. Pictish Voodoo Distributing Co., CA. 1993.

*―――. *Original Gardnerian Book of Shadows Documents.* Pictish Voodoo Distributing Co., CA. 1993.

Kerenyi, Carl. Eleusis: *Archetypal Image of Mother and Daughter.* Princeton University Press, Princeton, NJ. 1967.

Komroff, Manuel, ed. *The Apocrypha or Non-Canonical Books of the Bible.* Tudor Publishing Co., New York, NY. 1949.

Koppana, K. M. *Snakefat and Knotted Threads.* Mandragora Dimensions, Helsinki. 1990.

Lamb, Geoffrey. *Magic, Witchcraft and the Occult.* David and Charles, London. 1977.

Laycock, Donald C. *The Complete Enochian Dictionary.* Samuel Weiser, York Beach, ME. 1994.

Leach, Maria and Jerome Fried. *Funk and Wagnall's Standard Dictionary of Folklore, Mythology and Legend.* Funk and Wagnall's, New York, NY. 1972.

Lee, Bruce. *Tao of Jeet Kune Do.* Ohara Publications, Inc., Santa Clarita, CA. 1975.

Leek, Sybil. *Diary of a Witch.* New American Library, Inc., New York, NY. 1968.

―――. *Numerology, The Magic of Numbers.* Collier Macmillan Ltd. Toronto. 1969.

―――. *The Complete Art of Witchcraft.* World Publishing Co. New York, NY. 1971.

Legge, James. *The I Ching: The Book of Changes.* Dover Publications Inc., New York, NY. 1963.

Lehner, Ernst. *Symbols, Signs & Signets.* Dover Publications, Inc., New York, NY. 1950.

Leland, Charles Geoffrey. *Aradia: Gospel of the Witches.* Samuel Weiser, New York, NY. 1974.

Levi, Eliphas. *Transcendental Magic.* Samuel Weiser, Inc., New York, NY. 1974.

Lindsay, Jack. *The Ancient World: Manners and Morals.* Weidenfeld and Nicolson, London. 1968.

Loomis, Roger Sherman and Laura Hibbard Loomis. *Medieval Romances.* Random House, Inc., New York, NY. 1957.

Mac Cana, Proinsias. *Celtic Mythology.* Peter Bedrick Books, New York, NY. 1983.

MacDonald, Margaret Read, ed. *The Folklore of World Holidays.* Gale Research, Detroit, MI. 1992.

MacFarlane, A. D. J. *Witchcraft in Tudor and Stuart England.* Harper & Row, New York, NY. 1970.

MacKenzie, Kenneth R. H., ed. *Royal Masonic Cyclopedia.* Aquarian Press, New York, NY. 1987.

MacLennan, Malcolm. *Gaelic Dictionary.* Acair & Aberdeen University Press, Edinburgh. 1988.

Markale, Jean. *The Celts: Uncovering the Mythic and Historic Origins of Western Culture.* Inner Traditions International, Rochester, VT. 1993.

Marron, Kevin. *Witches, Pagans & Magic in the New Age.* McClelland-Gantam, Inc. Toronto. 1989.

Mathers, S. Liddell MacGregor, trans. *The Book of the Goetia, or The Lesser Key of Solomon.* Health Research, Mokelumne Hill, CA. 1976.

———. trans. *The Book of the Sacred Magic of Abramelin the Mage.* Dover Publications, Inc., New York, NY. 1975.

———. trans. *The Greater Key of Solomon.* DeLaurence Co., Chicago, IL. 1914.

Matthews, Caitlin. *Mabon and the Mysteries of Britain: An Exploration of the Mabinogion.* Routledge & Kegan Paul Ltd., New York, NY. 1987.

————. *The Elements of the Celtic Tradition.* Element, Inc. Rockport, MA. 1989.

Matthews, John. *Boadicea: Warrior Queen of the Celts.* Firebird Books, Poole, Dorset. 1988.

Matthews, John and Caitlin Matthews. *British & Irish Mythology: An Encylopedia of Myth and Legend.* Aquarian Press, London. 1988.

Matthews, John. *Fionn Mac Cumhail: Champion of Ireland.* Firebird Books, Poole, Dorset. 1988.

Matthiessen, Welhelm. *Folk Tales.* Grove Press, Inc., New York, NY. 1968.

*McFarland, Phoenix. *The Complete Book of Magical Names.* Llewellyn Publications, St. Paul, MN. 1995.

Metraux, Alfred. *Voodoo in Haiti.* Schocken Books, New York, NY. 1972.

Michelet, Jules. *Satanism and Witchcraft.* Citadel Press, New York, NY. 1939.

Millman, Dan. *The Way of the Peaceful Warrior: A Book That Changes Lives.* H. J. Kramer, Inc., Tiburton, CA. 1984.

Moonstone, Rowan. "The Origins of Halloween," *CultWatch Response,* Vol.I. Issue 1. CultWatch Response, Inc., Colorado Springs, CO. 1988

Moore, Robert and Douglas Gillette. *King, Warrior, Magician, Lover: Rediscovering the Archetypes of the Mature Masculine.* HarperCollins, San Francisco, CA. 1990.

————. *The Warrior Within: Accessing the Knight in the Male Psyche.* HarperCollins, San Francisco, CA. 1992.

Morris, Desmond. *The Naked Ape.* Corgi Books, London. 1967.

Mossman, Jennifer, ed. *Holidays and Anniversaries of the World.* Second Edition, Gale Research, Detroit, MI. 1990.

Mumford, Jonn. *Sexual Occultism.* Llewellyn Publications, St. Paul, MN. 1975.

Murray, Elaine. *A Layman's Guide to New Age and Spiritual Terms.* Blue Dolphin Publishing, Nevada City, CA. 1993.

Musashi, Miyamoto. *The Book of Five Rings.* Bantam Books, New York, NY. 1982.

Nitobe, Inazo. *Bushido: The Warrior's Code.* Ohara Publications, Inc., Burbank, CA. 1975.

Neumann, Erich. *The Great Mother: An Analysis of the Archetype.* Princeton University Press, New York, NY. 1963.

O'Faolain, Julia and Lauro Martines. *Not In God's Image.* Harper & Row, Publishers, San Francisco, CA. 1973.

Parker, Derek and Julia Parker. *The Compleat Astrologer.* Bantam Books, New York, NY. 1975.

Pennick, Nigel. *Magical Alphabets.* Samuel Weiser, York Beach, ME. 1992.

*Pennick, Nigel. *The Pagan Book of Days.* Destiny Books, Rochester, VT. 1992.

*Piggott, Stuart. *The Druids.* Thames & Hudson, New York, NY. 1975.

Prisig, Robert M. *Zen and the Art of Motorcycle Maintenance.* Bantam Books, New York, NY. 1974.

Proteus Coven. "The Protean Book of Shadows", Proteus Coven, New York, NY. 1995.

Radford, E. and M.A. Radford. *Encyclopedia of Superstitions.* Greenwood Press Publishers, Westport, CT. 1891.

Radice, Betty, trans. *The Letters of the Younger Pliny.* Penguin Books, London. 1969.

Ravenwolf, Silver. *To Ride a Silver Broomstick: New Generation Witchcraft.* Llewellyn Publications, St. Paul, MN. 1993.

Reader's Digest Association, ed. *Folklore, Myths and Legends of Britain.* Reader's Digest Association, London. 1977.

Reed, Ellen Cannon. *The Witches' Qabala.* Llewellyn Publications, St. Paul, MN. 1986.

Regardie, Israel, ed. *Gems From The Equinox: Instructions by Aleister Crowley for His Own Magical Order.* New Falcon Publications, Scottsdale, AZ. 1982.

————. *The Complete Golden Dawn System of Magic.* New Falcon Publications, Scottsdale, AZ. 1990.

Reuben, Gabriel H. and Sheila Schwartz. *How People Lived in Ancient Greece and Rome.* Benefic Press, Chicago, IL. 1974.

Rigaud, Milo. *Secrets of Voodoo.* City Lights Books, San Francisco, CA. 1985.

Robbins, Russell Hope. *The Encyclopedia of Witchcraft and Demonology.* Crown Publishers, New York, NY. 1973.

Roberts, J. M. *The Penguin History of the World.* Penguin Books, Harmondsworth, Middlesex. 1990.

Roberts, Jane. *The Nature of Personal Reality.* Bantam Books, New York, NY. 1974.

Robinson, Herbert Spencer and Knox Wilson. *Myths and Legends of All Nations.* Littlefield Adams Quality Paperbacks, Savage, MD. 1976.

Rolleston, T. W. *Celtic Myths and Legends.* Dover Publications, New York, NY. 1990.

*Russell, Jeffrey B. *A History of Witchcraft.* Thames & Hudson, London. 1980.

*Ryall, Rhiannon. *West Country Wicca.* Phoenix Publishing Inc., Custer, WA. 1989.

Sadhu, Mouni. *Concentration: A Guide to Mental Mastery.* Wilshire Book Co. North Hollywood, CA. 1959.

Saggs, H. W. F. *Civilization Before Greece and Rome.* Yale University Press, New Haven, CT. 1989.

*Sanders, Alex. *The Alex Sanders Lectures.* Magical Childe Publishing, Inc., New York, NY. 1984.

Sato, Giei. *Unsui: A Diary of Zen Monastic Life.* University of Hawaii Press, Honolulu, HI. 1973.

Schultes, Richard E. and Albert Hofmann. *Plants of the Gods: Their Sacred. Healing and Hallucinogenic Powers.* Healing Arts Press, Rochester, VT. 1992.

Sekida, Katsuki. *Zen Training: Methods and Philosophy.* John Weatherhill, Inc., New York, NY. 1975.

Sharkey, John. *Celtic Mysteries: The Ancient Religion.* Thames & Hudson, London. 1975.

Sharman-Burke, Juliet and Liz Greene. *The Mythic Tarot.* Simon & Schuster, Inc., New York, NY. 1986.

Sharman-Burke, Juliet. *The Mythic Tarot Workbook.* Simon & Schuster, Inc., New York, NY. 1988.

Shepard, Leslie, ed. *Encyclopedia of Occultism and Parapsychology, Vols 1-3.* Gale Research Co., Detroit, MI.

Shepherd, Cybill and Paula Yoo. (29 June 1998). "Meno-Peace: A Star Discovers That The Change Of Life Need Not Be One For The Worse," *People* magazine, Volume 49, No. 25, p. 74.

Sherwin-White, N. *Ancient Rome.* Longman Group, Ltd., London. 1959.

*Skelton, Robin. *Spellcraft.* McClelland & Stewart, Toronto. 1978.

*———. *The Practice of Witchcraft.* Robert Hale Ltd., Custer, WA. 1988.

Sprenger, Johann and Heinrich Kramer. *Malleus Maleficarum.* Benjamin Blom, Inc., New York, NY. 1928.

Squire, Charles. *Celtic Myth and Legend.* Newcastle Publishing, Inc., North Hollywood, CA. 1975.

Starhawk. *Dreaming the Dark: Magic, Sex and Politics.* Beacon Press, Boston, MA. 1982.

*———. *The Spiral Dance: A Rebirth of the Ancient Religion of the Great Goddess.* Harper & Row, New York, NY. 1979.

———. *Truth or Dare?* Beacon Press, Boston, MA. 1987

Stewart, Bob. *Cuchulainn: Hound of Ulster.* Firebird Books, Poole, Dorset. 1988.

———. *Macbeth: Scotland's Warrior King.* Firebird Books, Poole, Dorset. 1988.

*Stewart, R. J. *Celtic Gods, Celtic Goddesses.* Blandford, London. 1990.

———. *The Spiritual Dimension of Music.* Destiny Books, Rochester, VT. 1986.

Stone, Merlin. *When God Was A Woman.* Harcourt, Brace Jovanovich, Publishers, New York, NY. 1976.

Summers, Montague. *The History of Witchcraft and Demonology.* Routledge and Kegan Paul Ltd., New York, NY. 1965.

Symonds, John, ed. *The Confessions of Aleister Crowley.* Arkana, London. 1979.

Thorsson, Edred. *Northern Magic.* Llewellyn Publications, St. Paul, MN. 1992.

Three Initiates. *The Kybalion.* Yogi Publication Society, Chicago, IL. 1940.

Trungpa, Chogyam. *Shambhala: The Sacred Path of the Warrior.* Shambhala, Boston, MA. 1984.

Turner, Robert. *Elizabethan Magic: The Art and the Magus.* Element Books, Shaftesbury, Dorset. 1989.

Tyson, Donald, ed. *Three Books of Occult Philosophy: Henry Cornelius Agrippa of Nettesheim.* Llewellyn, St. Paul, MN. 1993.

Tzu, Sun. Cleary, Thomas, trans. *The Art of War.* Shambhala, Boston, MA. 1991.

Underwood, Peter. *Dictionary of the Supernatural.* Harrap, London. 1978.

U. S. Government Publication #008-020-00745-5. *Religious Requirements of Certain Selected Groups—a Handbook for Chaplains.* Kirschner Associates, Inc.

*Valiente, Doreen. *An ABC of Witchcraft.* Phoenix Publishing, Custer, WA. 1973.

*———. *Natural Magic.* Phoenix Publishing, Custer, WA. 1986.

*———. *Witchcraft For Tomorrow.* Phoenix Publishing, Custer, WA. 1978.

Waite, Arthur Edward. *The Book of Black Magic and Ceremonial Magic.* Causeway Books, New York, NY. 1973.

Walker, Barbara. *The Skeptical Feminist.* Harper & Row, San Francisco, CA. 1987.

———. *The Woman's Encyclopedia of Myths and Secrets.* HarperCollins, San Francisco, CA. 1983.

———. *The Women's Encyclopedia of Symbols and Sacred Objects.* HarperCollins, San Francisco, CA. 1988.

Waring, Philippa. *A Dictionary of Omens and Superstitions.* Ballantine Books, New York, NY. 1978.

Wedeck, H. E. and W. Baskin. *Dictionary of Spiritualism.* Peter Owen, London. 1971.

Wedge, Tom. "Seminar Package on Occult Crime." Bellefontaine, OH. 1982.

Weiner, Bernard. *Boy Into Man: A Father's Guide to Initiation of Teenage Sons.* Transformation Press, San Francisco, CA. 1992.

*Weinstein, Marion. *Earth Magic: A Dianic Book of Shadows.* Phoenix Publishing, Custer, WA. 1980.

*———. *Positive Magic.* Phoenix Publishing, Custer, WA. 1978.

Wentz, W. Y. Evans. *The Fairy Faith in Celtic Countries.* Oxford University Press, Oxford. 1911.

Wiehl, Andrew. *Creative Visualization.* Llewellyn Publications, St. Paul, MN. 1958.

Wilcox, Laird (ed.). *Guide to the American Occult—Directory & Bibliography* 1988. Priority One Consultants, Orange, NJ. 1988

Wilson, Colin. *The Occult: A History.* Random House, New York, NY. 1971.

*Worth, Valerie. *The Crone's Book of Words.* Llewellyn Publications, St. Paul, MN. 1986.

Manuscripts

Georgian Book of Shadows. author's handwritten copy from Circle of Amergin, Vancouver, BC. 1990.

NROOGD Book of Shadows. Circle of Amergin, Vancouver, BC. 1990.

INDEX

☽ REACH FOR THE MOON

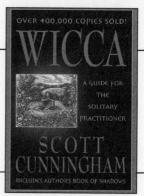

Wicca
A Guide for the Solitary Practitioner

Scott Cunningham

Wicca is a book of life, and how to live magically, spiritually, and wholly attuned with Nature. It is a book of sense and common sense, not only about Magick, but about religion and one of the most critical issues of today: how to achieve the much needed and wholesome relationship with our Earth. Cunningham presents Wicca as it is today: a gentle, Earth-oriented religion dedicated to the Goddess and God. This book fulfills a need for a practical guide to solitary Wicca—a need which no previous book has fulfilled.

Here is a positive, practical introduction to the religion of Wicca, designed so that any interested person can learn to practice the religion alone, anywhere in the world. It presents Wicca honestly and clearly, without the pseudo-history that permeates other books. It shows that Wicca is a vital, satisfying part of twentieth century life.

This book presents the theory and practice of Wicca from an individual's perspective. The section on the Standing Stones Book of Shadows contains solitary rituals for the Esbats and Sabbats. This book, based on the author's nearly two decades of Wiccan practice, presents an eclectic picture of various aspects of this religion. Exercises designed to develop magical proficiency, a self-dedication ritual, herb, crystal and rune magic, as well as recipes for Sabbat feasts, are included in this excellent book.

0-87542-118-0, 6 x 9, 240 pp., illus., softcover   **$9.95**

The Complete Book of Magical Names

Phoenix McFarland

There is a tremendous energy within names—the ancients understood this and chose their names carefully. This book explains how you can use names as the magical tools of self-transformation that they are. Select that special name that reflects who you truly are and take a giant step towards personal empowerment!

More than just a thorough study of the history of names and nomenclature—this book is the only lexicon of non-Christian names and their meanings in print. Written from a Wiccan perspective by a practicing priestess, this book contains nearly 5,000 names (including pronunciations) taken from modern and ancient sources: nature, mythology, history, fantasy literature, folklore, and faraway lands. Names are indexed alphabetically and by the characteristics they invoke for ease of use.

Discover the folklore behind your name, and learn specific rituals to unleash the power within names. Create new and unique names for anything, or anyone, from your coven to your cat. A thoughtful gift for initiations, handfastings, and baby showers.

1-56718-251-8, 7 x 10, 320 pp., illus., softcover   **$19.95**

Ancient Ways
Reclaiming the Pagan Tradition

Pauline Campanelli

Ancient Ways is filled with magick and ritual that you can perform every day to capture the spirit of the seasons. It focuses on the celebration of the Sabbats of the Old Religion by giving you practical things to do while anticipating the sabbat rites, and helping you harness the magical energy for weeks afterward. The wealth of seasonal rituals and charms are drawn from ancient sources but are easily performed with materials readily available.

Learn how to look into your previous lives at Yule . . . at Beltane, discover the places where you are most likely to see faeries . . . make special jewelry to wear for your Lammas Celebrations . . . for the special animals in your life, paint a charm of protection at Midsummer.

Most Pagans and Wiccans feel that the Sabbat rituals are all too brief and wish for the magick to linger on. *Ancient Ways* can help you reclaim your own traditions and heighten the feeling of magick.

0-87542-090-7, 7 x 10, 256 pp., illus., softcover   **$14.95**

Living Wicca
A Further Guide for the Solitary Practitioner

Scott Cunningham

Living Wicca is the long-awaited sequel to Scott Cunningham's wildly successful *Wicca: a Guide for the Solitary Practitioner*. This book is for those who have made the conscious decision to bring their Wiccan spirituality into their everyday lives. It provides solitary practitioners with the tools and added insights that will enable them to blaze their own spiritual paths—to become their own high priests and priestesses.

Living Wicca takes a philosophical look at the questions, practices, and differences within Witchcraft. It covers the various tools of learning available to the practitioner, the importance of secrecy in one's practice, guidelines to performing ritual when ill, magical names, initiation, and the Mysteries. It discusses the benefits of daily prayer and meditation, making offerings to the gods, how to develop a prayerful attitude, and how to perform Wiccan rites when away from home or in emergency situations.

Unlike any other book on the subject, *Living Wicca* is a step-by-step guide to creating your own Wiccan tradition and personal vision of the gods, designing your personal ritual and symbols, developing your own book of shadows, and truly living your Craft.

0-87542-184-9, 208 pp., 6 x 9, illus. **$12.95**

Hereditary Witchcraft
Secrets of the Old Religion

Raven Grimassi

This book is about the Old Religion of Italy, and contains material that is at least 100 years old, much of which has never before been seen in print. This overview of the history and lore of the Hereditary Craft will show you how the Italian witches viewed nature, magick, and the occult forces. Nothing in this book is mixed with, or drawn from, any other Wiccan traditions.

The Italian witches would gather beneath the full moon to worship a goddess (Diana) and a god (Dianus). The roots of Italian Witchcraft extend back into the pre-history of Italy, in the indigenous Mediterranean/Aegean neolithic cult of the Great Goddess. Follow its development to the time of the Inquisition, when it had to go into hiding to survive, and to the present day. Uncover surprising discoveries of how expressions of Italian Witchcraft have been taught and used in this century.

1-56718-256-9, 7 1/2 x 9 1/8, 288 pp., 31 illus., softcover　　　　　**$14.95**

Wiccan Magick
Inner Teachings of the Craft

Raven Grimassi

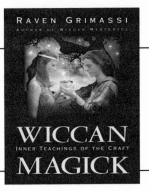

Wiccan Magick is a serious and complete study for those who desire to understand the inner meanings, techniques and symbolism of magick as an occult art. Magick within modern Wicca is an eclectic blending of many occult traditions that evolved from the ancient beliefs and practices in both Europe, the Middle East, and Asia. *Wiccan Magick* covers the full range of magickal and ritual practices as they pertain to both modern ceremonial and shamanic Wicca.

Come to understand the evolution of the Craft, the ancient magickal current that flows from the past to the present, and the various aspects included in ritual, spell casting, and general theology. When you understand why something exists within a ritual structure, you will know better how to build upon the underlying concepts to create ritual that is meaningful to you.

1-56718-255-0, 6 x 9, 240 pp., softcover   **$12.95**

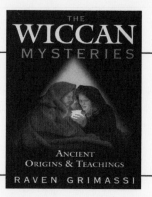

The Wiccan Mysteries
Ancient Origins & Teachings

Raven Grimassi

What you will encounter in *The Wiccan Mysteries* is material that was once taught only in the initiate levels of the old Wiccan Mystery Traditions, and to which many solitary practitioners have never had access. Learn the inner meanings of Wiccan rites, beliefs and practices, and discover the time-proven concepts that created, maintained and carried Wiccan beliefs up into this modern era. In reflecting back upon the wisdom of our ancestors, neo-Wiccans can draw even greater sustenance from the spiritual stores of Wicca—the Old Religion.

The Wiccan Mysteries will challenge you to expand your understanding and even re-examine your own perceptions. Wicca is essentially a Celtic-oriented religion, but its Mystery Tradition is derived from several outside cultures as well. You will come away with a sense of the rich heritage that was passed from one human community to another, and that now resides within this system for spiritual development.

1-56718-254-2, 6 x 9, 312 pp., softcover   **$14.95**

Wheel of the Year
Living the Magical Life

Pauline Campanelli

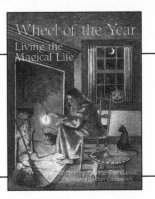

If you feel elated by the celebrations of the Sabbats and hunger for that feeling during the long weeks between Sabbats, *Wheel of the Year* can help you put the joy and fulfillment of magic into your everyday life. This book shows you how to celebrate the lesser changes in Nature. The wealth of seasonal rituals and charms are all easily performed with materials readily available and are simple and concise enough that the practitioner can easily adapt them to work within the framework of his or her own Pagan tradition.

Learn to perform fire magic in November, the secret Pagan symbolism of Christmas tree ornaments, the best time to visit a fairy forest or sacred spring and what to do when you get there. Learn the charms and rituals and the making of magical tools that coincide with the nesting season of migratory birds. Whether you are a newcomer to the Craft or have found your way back many years ago, *Wheel of the Year* will be an invaluable reference book in your practical magic library. It is filled with magic and ritual for everyday life and will enhance any system of Pagan Ritual.

0-87542-091-5, 7 x 10, 176 pp., illus., softcover   **$12.95**

True Magick
A Beginner's Guide

Amber K

True Magick can change your life. With magick's aid, you can have vibrant health, prosperity or a new career. You can enhance your relationships or bring new ones into your life. With magick, you can reach deep inside yourself to find confidence, courage, tranquility, faith, compassion, understanding or humor. If you're curious about magick, you will find answers in this book. Amber K, a High Priestess of the Wiccan religion and experienced practitioner of magick, explains not only the history and lore of magick, but also its major varieties in the world today. And if you want to practice magick, then this book will start you on the path.

0-87542-003-6, 272 pp., mass market, illus.　　　　　　　　**$4.95**

To order, call 1-800-THE MOON
Prices subject to change without notice

Buckland's Complete Book of Witchcraft

Raymond Buckland

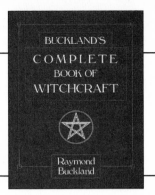

Here is the most complete resource to the study and practice of modern, non-denominational Wicca. This is a lavishly illustrated, self-study course for the solitary or group. Included are rituals; exercises for developing psychic talents; information on all major "sects" of the Craft; sections on tools, beliefs, dreams, meditations, divination, herbal lore, healing, ritual clothing and much, much more. This book unites theory and practice into a comprehensive course designed to help you develop into a practicing Witch, one of the "Wise Ones." It is written by Ray Buckland, a very famous and respected authority on Witchcraft who first came public with the Old Religion in the United States. Large format with workbook-type exercises, profusely illustrated and full of music and chants. Takes you from A to Z in the study of Witchcraft.

Never before has so much information on the Craft of the Wise been collected in one place. Traditionally, there are three degrees of advancement in most Wiccan traditions. When you have completed studying this book, you will be the equivalent of a Third-Degree Witch. Even those who have practiced Wicca for years find useful information in this book, and many covens are using this for their textbook. If you want to become a Witch, or if you merely want to find out what Witchcraft is really about, you will find no better book than this.

0-87542-050-8, 8 ¹/₂ x 11, 272 pp., illus., softcover   **$16.95**

Magical Rites from the Crystal Well
A Classic Text for Wiccans & Pagans

Ed Fitch

In nature, and in the earth, we look and find beauty. Within ourselves we find a well from which we may draw truth and knowledge. And when we draw from this well, we rediscover that we are all children of the Earth.

The simple rites in this book are presented to you as a means of finding your own way back to nature; for discovering and experiencing the beauty and the magic of unity with the source. These are the celebrations of the seasons; at the same time they are rites by which we attune ourselves to the flow of the force: the energy of life.

These are rites of passage by which we celebrate the major transitions we all experience in life. Here are the Old Ways, but they are also the Ways for Today.

0-87542-230-6, 7 x 10, 160 pp., illus., softcover   **$12.95**

The Crone's Book of Magical Words

Valerie Worth

Crone's Book of Magical Words contains rituals and spells to avert temptation, win another's love, recall one who is unfaithful, overcome insomnia, seek that which has been lost, atone for cutting down a tree, train a familiar, see the future, keep hair from falling, defeat tobacco, bring rain, and much more. Magic is alive, and Magic is afoot in the world today in the words spoken, read, sung, or only imagined. Here is Magic to enjoy and use: Magic to shape reality according to human will. Here is not the Magic of ceremony, of expensive robes and complex paraphernalia, nor of formulae calling for ingredients from the far ends of earth. This Magic is from the heart, this Magic sings in a woman's voice and is shaped with a woman's hands; it is the Magic incarnate in every woman for every woman knows of the Power within.

Valerie Worth—poet, wise woman, student of the occult—has created from her studies of Nature, Folklore and Magic these poems that are instructions, incantations and spells for nearly every purpose, from the personal to the universal. She bases her work on certain premises: that words themselves are a means to control exterior phenomena and interior changes; that magic today is the same craft that it has always been; and that all rituals spring from the same vision of life made meaningful.

1-56718-825-7, 5 ³/₁₆ x 8, 168 pp., illus., softcover   **$7.95**

Covencraft
Witchcraft for Three or More

Amber K

Here is the complete guidebook for anyone who desires to practice Witchcraft in a caring, challenging, well-organized spiritual support group: a coven. Whether you hope to learn more about this ancient spiritual path . . . are a coven member wanting more rewarding experiences in your group . . . are looking for a coven to join, or are thinking of starting one . . . or are a Wiccan elder gathering proven techniques and fresh ideas . . . this book is for you.

Amber K shares what she as learned about beginning and maintaining healthy covens in her 20 years as a Wiccan priestess. Learn what a coven is, how it works, and how you can make your coven experience more effective, enjoyable and rewarding. Plus, get practical hands-on guidance in the form of sample Articles of Incorporation, internet resources, sample by-laws, and sample budgets. Seventeen ritual scripts are also provided.

1-56718-018-3, 7 x 10, 480 pp., illus., softcover   **$17.95**